GLOW OF CANDLELIGHT

PATRICIA MURPHY

Portrait by Jon Whitcomb

GLOW OF CANDLELIGHT

The Story of Patricia Murphy

by Patricia Murphy

Prentice-Hall, Inc., Englewood Cliffs, N.J.

Library of Congress Catalogue Card Number 61-15517

Printed in the United States of America

35747—T

Dedication

to

The two most important people in my life—

my husband and my mother.

ACKNOWLEDGMENT

I WISH TO thank the following for their unfailing and valuable collaboration on this volume:

Howard Barnes and Katherine Vincent Barnes, whose understanding and expert literary aid made the memoirs possible; Demetria Taylor, Home Economist, for testing and setting down in recipe form for home use the many treats in the food section; John Rebhan, authority on horticulture, who has understood so well my feeling about flowers; John E. Rogers, General Manager of the restaurants; Gregory D. Camilluci, who manages the Fort Lauderdale Candlelight; William Ellis, who drove us all over, morning, noon and night, so cheerfully; Dr. Arthur H. Kaupe of Palm Beach, Florida; Dr. J. J. Mitroff of New York City, who put up with my annual winter pastime—pneumonia—and got me over it; David Fishstein, without whose encouragement and moral support this book could not have happened.

Wilma Freeman, valued friend and agent, who envisioned and implemented the entire work, editing, organizing, and encouraging all of us.

PREFACE

MANY FRAGMENTS HAVE been written about Patricia Murphy—the woman who ran a tea room into a million dollar business, the lady with a green thumb who wins prizes at flower shows, the New York and Florida hostess, who gives parties by the sea, the collector of curious gifts from all corners of the world, who makes them available to everyone visiting her gift shops.

Yet, I have always thought there was nothing unusual about my life; no earth-shaking melodrama, nothing of political or international import; no truly artistic achievement.

But then I married, and my husband, Captain James E. Kiernan, was a very wonderful man and we had ten of the happiest and busiest years a couple could have. When he died I thought the world had ended for me. For months and months, I cared about nothing, not even my business. Then I realized that this was not as he would have wished it. Slowly I started reviewing the things we had planned together and, as I regained physical and spiritual strength, I determined to carry through our many projects.

One of these projects was this book.

In an affectionate, jovial mood, my husband used to say: "Pat, you're a real Horatio Alger character—a little girl from a small Newfoundland village, barging into New York in the depression and making millions in one of the toughest businesses around. You're a real live, exciting success story."

But in a more serious mood he would urge me to reconstruct my life and career as a sort of guide for people who were on the threshold of endeavor, in whatever fields. For, as Captain Kiernan said:

"You've used no secret formulas, Pat, in becoming a legend in your own time. You've just slugged away. No matter what the odds, trying to give people a sense of gracious living, trying to make them see that even without great wealth or celebrity the average person can derive great satisfaction out of such simple things as good food, flowers, lovely gifts, beautiful surroundings. You have no secret formulas, but you know how to do it. Pass the word along."

While he was alive I steadfastly resisted any impulse to look into myself, to try to discover the things that had made Patricia Murphy what she was. But now I think he was right. In any case, here is my story. Perhaps it may help others who, starting with little, are seeking much.

Patricia Murphy

CONTENTS

PART I MY LIFE

PART II GARDENS AND FLOWERS

PART III MY FAVORITE FOODS AND MENUS

Part I
MY LIFE

Chapter One

FAR-FLUNG CANDLELIGHT

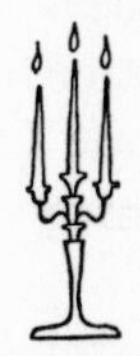

As I write, images and fragments of conversation crowd my mind. A picture of a tiny Newfoundlander opening a little, hex-ridden restaurant in Brooklyn. A smiling chef serving heaping portions of good rich food on plate after plate as waitresses hurry piping-hot dishes to a thousand guests waiting at the Candlelight Restaurant in Westchester. The entrance to the New York Coliseum with its exhibit of my rare and beautiful flowers setting off the annual show. The elegant vista of a yacht-filled marina, and the owners of such splendid boats dining in my newest restaurant, the Bahia Mar Candlelight in Fort Lauderdale, Florida. The Westchester Candlelight at Christmas, beautifully decorated and crowded with people from all over, come to enjoy fine food and drink and to see the sparkling hillside, the crèche with live sheep, the reindeer.

There is the voice of Captain Kiernan, to whom I was married for ten years, saying:

"Pat, this planting of grass in little sprigs is going to be terribly expensive. Why can't we just paint the sand green?"

The lawn is beautiful here at my Florida home, "Kinsale," running down to the lagoon and circling the swimming pool and the rocky slope with winding paths that give one the illusion of being on a high promontory, although the elevation is really very slight. Captain Kiernan and I used to sit on the terrace of the lovely house with its two towering white chimneys. It is a particularly enchanting part of the Florida coast outside Stuart, thirty-seven miles north of Palm Beach. Beyond the lagoon there is a tree-filled island. Beyond that, the great bay and the vast Atlantic Ocean. At dusk hidden spotlights come on to pick up stately palms, hibiscus, orchids and rare flowering vines.

This is my real home, although I spend much of my time in "Sky High," a lofty penthouse on upper Fifth Avenue, New York, overlooking both the Hudson and East Rivers. Fortunately, I can now spend far more time at Kinsale without that terrible feeling of urgency, which has been with me as long as I can remember, forcing me into a merry-go-round of feverish activity. For my lovely Florida home, the marble cabana and swimming pool, the creek with a bridge, the greenhouses, the lagoon and the island beyond are close to my Marina Candlelight, in Fort Lauderdale, a reasonable drive, or a few minutes in my Cessna private plane. This is what my husband, Rosie, wanted for me. It makes me very sad that he did not live to see his carefully-laid plans for my enjoyment of living come to fruition. For a long time after his death I did not think I could enjoy life on any terms.

But much of my time is still governed by urgency. Anyone who thinks that running restaurants—satisfying the "inner man" of a vast public while keeping the "outer man" relaxed and happy—is an easy job should stay away from the business. It is a great gamble; it is nerve-racking as a personal involvement. After many years I think I know some of the answers. Otherwise my Westchester Candlelight, where 10,000 people have been served on a holiday and about a million during a year, wouldn't be worth $4,000,000 today after having once been called "Murphy's Folly." My Bahia Mar Candlelight in Fort Lauderdale, much smaller, serves over two thousand diners daily, turning hundreds of others away. And with the flowers, gifts, and Patricia Murphy perfumes sold in both places, a little restaurant in Brooklyn has grown into quite a business.

What Rosie did for me was to teach me to turn part of my energies into private pleasure and satisfaction. Anyone who has visited Kinsale will tell you that it is a breath-taking experience—not only because of the exotic flowers, lawns, lighting and the house and cabana, but also because it is serenely beautiful in its perfect setting. Garden clubs have been fascinated by my plantings on the huge terraces of Sky High, my New York penthouse, finding everything on display from orchids to an herb garden.

It may surprise you to learn that flying my own plane has given me one of the deepest personal satisfactions I have had since I was able to stop working twelve to fifteen hours a day. It is not, I think, what Rosie would have wished me to do. For he was always working, unobtrusively, to lessen the many tensions I was inevitably under in my business. But with his great tradition of the Navy and the challenge of the unknown, he would have understood that the stunning grief I felt after he was cut off in his prime could only have been tempered for me by trying something utterly new and different—like flying.

I was afraid of flying at first, as anyone in his right mind should be. I was no wild-eyed youngster looking for kicks, and I made sure that my two-engined Cessna was equipped with every safety device known. And soaring high over the Florida coast or winging into Westchester while shuttling back and forth between my two restaurants, I was closer to Rosie and my memories of him than I had ever been since the tragedy of his passing.

On the practical side, my airplane saves endless time in my

restaurant management and allows me to make magical shifts of personnel, food, flowers and gifts to meet the changing seasons in two widely separated and vastly different regions of the country. My personal pilot, Alexander Cabana, Jr., who is vastly complimentary about my skill as an aviatrix, flew jet fighters in the Korean War. I have often thought he must have been equally courageous when I started handling the controls of the first small plane in which we flew.

There are many badges of success—money itself, the vast credit that is assured by successful business activity, houses, swimming pools, fine automobiles, show horses, beautiful clothes, even a private plane, but the awards for my flowers and work in horticulture are dearer to me than most of the material benefits of my business. Perhaps this is because I spent my impressionable girlhood on a barren rock-strewn coast of Newfoundland. My dear mother, whom I have always called Nana, loves flowers.

I remember gathering moss, seaweed, and anything else that would turn into growing soil and bringing it to her little garden in Newfoundland. Like so many women of Irish and Welsh descent, she has a green thumb and she had her little garden full of blooms. It was a unique sight in Placentia, the fishing village where I grew up. I must have inherited the green thumb; I certainly inherited a fierce love of flowers and plants.

Even in the early days of my restaurant business I would spend precious cash on greenery and flowers and I cherished any spot of city ground where a tree would grow. It took me twenty years to have a garden of my own, but I'm certain that flowers have had a large part in my success and they have given me the deepest personal satisfaction. Whenever I look at the hillside I transformed from an unsightly, rocky eight acres into a lush expanse of 50,000 tulips coming into bloom, to be followed by a profusion of other blooms throughout summer and fall at the Westchester Candlelight, I feel a surge of delight.

"NANA"

CAPTAIN JAMES E. KIERNAN

The same is true when I see the more than 100,000 orchid plants I have in my seven greenhouses and the many, many more growing in their natural habitat at Kinsale in Florida.

One word about the so-called green thumb. Some people have a knack with growing things, a sort of instinct about handling them, watering them and caring for them, and I am one of these. But most of my success with flowers and plants, from the common geranium or hardy begonia to orchids and hibiscus has been the result of hard work. So I'll go on record as saying that the green thumb is nine-tenths muscle.

When I started in with orchids, for instance, Rosie found me weighted down by a volume of the Bailey Encyclopedia.

"What in the world are you looking up, Pat?" he asked.

"I'm not 'looking up' anything," I answered. "I'm just learning everything I can about orchids."

And hours were spent in reading as well as experimenting in greenhouses and at Kinsale before I considered myself even a fair amateur in orchid culture. Actually what I consider one of my most exciting horticultural experiments is the work I have done in acclimating supposed temperate plants to semi-tropical Florida and reversing the process. So much of good gardening is a matter of doing, of trial and error, of daring and imagination, that all of us can find great satisfaction in the small victories we achieve.

My culinary interests can scarcely be attributed to natural instinct. As a small girl I loved to invade the kitchen, but I'm told that my concoctions, while vastly ambitious, were not rousingly successful. From the start of my restaurant career I read everything I could lay my hands on. Popovers have been a sort of trade-mark of my Candlelight dining rooms, but popovers did not occur to me in a blinding flash. I went through lists of hot breads, knowing that hot bread was an item that people who were dining out were not likely to have at home. I rejected all sorts of buns, muffins and rolls, and chose my popovers because they were tasty, slightly exotic and not too hard to make. I love the dishes of many countries, and occasionally salute the U. N. with varied foreign dishes at my Candlelight. But on the whole I have tried to hold my menus to fine food well cooked.

No account of my present world would be complete without a mention of my London supper club at No. 6 Hamilton Place. Rosie and I acquired it, almost accidentally, over a weekend. London was his favorite city and we spent many weeks there before his death. One Saturday night, a friend of ours, Major Peter Anthony Davies, told us that the old Sir Victor Sassoon town house, which has a coat of arms in every panel of the library, had been turned into a supper club after having been used by a French cultural society. It was a lovely house in a wonderful district, but the restaurant was about to be liquidated for lack of funds and proper management.

We had to lay our hands on several thousand pounds before Monday morning, and unless you happen to have that sort of cash on your person it is difficult to secure it on a London Sunday morning. Fortunately, Rosie knew someone high up at Barclay's Bank, and we raised the necessary amount.

There are dues of four pounds a year for members, of which there are many, so that the place is flourishing. I wish I could be there more often. Not long ago, when I leased a castle in Ireland for the summer, I was able to take a more active hand in managing it. But I always keep in touch regularly by trans-atlantic phone.

Well, there you have a glimpse of Eleanor Patricia Murphy Kiernan, restauratrice and business woman, horticulturist, horse-woman, aviatrix, hostess and world traveller . . . as the world sees her. But it is only a superficial portrait. Let me tell you what actually happened to the determined young woman who emigrated from a Newfoundland fishing village to New York during the fearful period of the Depression.

Chapter Two

JOURNEY TO BROOKLYN HEIGHTS

NEW YORK WILL always bring to my mind the picture of a tall, gaunt old man and a slight girl of eighteen standing outside a basement store on West 14th Street in the fateful year of 1929. The man was my great-uncle, Frank Murphy, of Staten Island. He was shaking with anger, but this did not daunt the diminutive miss beside him.

"We've looked at every hat in New York," he roared.

"We have not," I answered firmly, knowing instinctively that the greatest city in the world contained far greater millinery delights than I had seen on the shabby shopping thoroughfare. I crushed my old straw hat down on my head, arranging the bunch of cherries and streamers in the back. Reassuringly I felt the roll of bills in my pocketbook which my father had given me in Newfoundland before sending me to his uncle's home in New York, to study the piano.

"Well, then, we'll be going back to Staten Island," said my uncle exasperatedly.

I pursed my lips, smoothed my middy blouse and followed him to the Staten Island ferry. As my heels dug firmly into the pavement, one thought kept racing through my head:

"Staten Island is not for me."

Already a diabolical plan was forming. I would leave there tomorrow.

And I did.

It was a strange start on a new life for a young girl from a Newfoundland fishing village in a great and unknown city. But it has always seemed quite natural to me. I did not even seriously consider the sacrifice of a musical career, however well it might have developed. New York was definitely not going to mean Staten Island, 14th Street, or piano exercises.

There was one more break to be made from family security after leaving great-uncle Frank to his investments in Staten Island real estate. I visited my mother's former guardian, a doctor on West 52nd Street. He wanted no more part of me than did my great-uncle Frank. He grudgingly permitted me to sleep in the examining room at his office.

For a week I went to sleep each night amid the querulous echoes of sick people, with the ominous examining table beside my couch. Terrifying heads of big game trophies, bagged by the good doctor, glared at me from the walls. What a relief to escape early each morning and wander through New York, generally arriving at my favorite haunt, Morningside Heights, where I felt kinship with the Columbia students.

A week in Dr. Bagg's examining room was enough for me. I do not remember whether I was nudged out of this unpleasant refuge or merely up and left. I think I was urged politely to leave. In any case, I found myself in the Three Arts Club, where I squandered eight dollars in one luxurious week. More than that was out of the question, with my dwindling roll of American dollars.

Through a girl at Columbia, who had also emigrated to New

York from Newfoundland, I heard of a reasonable rooming house. When I found that a room was only $4 a week I left the Three Arts Club in a hurry.

I never understood how my Newfoundland girl friend made her way around. She was very defensive about being a "foreigner." She would never ask directions, even in a department store, for she was scared to death that she would be labeled an out-of-towner, though most of the people we were brushing against had been or were just that themselves.

As for me, I always asked the way—in the subway, on the old elevated, on the street, or in stores. I was definitely curious. I was always in a hurry in those days and I wanted to learn everything. After all, when an American goes to Rome, he is not embarrassed by not knowing the way to the Via Veneto or how much a lira is worth. And I was really confused by a lot of the goings-on in New York in those final months of what has been called the era of wonderful nonsense. I didn't like being confused.

Everybody seemed to be "in the market" and talked about fabulous "paper profits." I carefully put $60 in a savings bank, so that I could get back home to Newfoundland if I had to, and went job-hunting. It was not too difficult at first. Money was easy and people were friendly. Dance marathons were luring people to Madison Square Garden. Jimmy Walker was a "Beau Brummel mayor" with a high, wide and handsome administration. The movies were becoming "talkies"; crazy characters were sitting on flagpoles and women's skirts were very, very short. And society columns were full of the fabulous doings at a magic place called Central Park Casino.

My first work was really play—playing the piano in a students' cafeteria-restaurant near Columbia University, where young people ate, visited and relaxed. I played during the lunch hours. William C. Orth, who has had considerable success as a musician, took over in the evenings. He was very nice to me.

Running to work one day I knocked the heel off my shoe and was literally incapacitated, as I only had twenty-six cents in my bag. Bill Orth was on hand early and advanced me enough money to get "on my feet" again.

The pay wasn't much, as you've probably guessed, but I got my meals free. Then I discovered that if a member of the cafeteria staff didn't show up, I could earn something extra by getting behind the counter and dishing out the blue-plate specials. I would arrive at 6 A.M., although I didn't have to play until the lunch hour. At that early hour in the morning I had the best chance of filling in for missing people. My only trouble was that I couldn't play popular music. Chopin, Beethoven and even my own improvising was what the kids got with their lunch. With jazz sweeping the country I was in the wrong business, but for a time it made me feel as though I was pursuing the career I had originally had in mind when I came to New York.

What I really would have liked to be was a hostess; I used to practice escorting parties to their tables in the secrecy of my furnished room. But, of course, my five-foot height stopped me in this work before I even got through an interview. And besides, I looked far younger and less mature than my seventeen years.

So I fell back on hand-coloring postcards at $3 a hundred. It paid the rent but didn't give me much to eat on. As a matter of fact I didn't eat too much in those months before I started my own restaurant. I used all the tricks that youngsters employ when they're on their own, even munching dry raisins and then drinking a lot of water. You'd be surprised how this can fill you up.

Working in restaurants seemed to me a good way to insure survival, so I got a job as cashier in one of Mr. and Mrs. Foster's little restaurants. (There was one on Broadway at 86th Street, where I counted change, and another on 44th Street.)

I remember that there was a real Russian princess as hostess, who wouldn't give me time off to look at the St. Patrick's Day Parade in the spring of 1929. After my first week of work I found a pink envelope in the drawer where I kept my personal belongings. I had heard of pink envelopes and thought that I was fired, but I decided to get another good meal out of the job. I left the envelope and reported to work the next morning, catching an early free lunch before facing the music at the cashier's desk.

There was the Russian princess holding the pink envelope in her hand and shaking it in my face.

"Well, my Irish colleen, are you so rich that you don't need your weekly salary?"

With trembling hands, I opened the envelope and found $9, a half week's pay! The pink envelope was purely accidental. I worked very briefly at Mr. and Mrs. Foster's, but I ate well and saved a little money, which I was going to need in the terrible fall ahead. My undoing was partly ignorance, partly misplaced zeal. You see, the dinner was a standard 70¢ (no sales tax in those days). I knew that the proper change for a dollar bill was three dimes, and kept accounts all right, but it never occurred to me that I could also have given quarters and nickels in change. The proprietors thought my reliance on dimes showed a lack of business experience.

Moreover, I really wanted to make the little restaurant succeed, so I appointed myself a saleslady of trifles at the desk. Departing diners would be importuned to buy chocolate bars, chewing gum, cigarettes. I was remarkably successful, but Mr. Foster thought it was bad form to push the Tootsie Rolls and Sweet Caporal cigarettes. Added to my ignorance of change-making, my sales efforts were frowned on, and for a second time I failed to enter the restaurant business at the lowest possible level.

It was a bad time to lose a job. The stock market crash didn't seem important to me at the time. I was worried about my $60 in the savings bank, but once I discovered that this was safe, New York was still a great adventure and challenge. There were always postcards to hand-color, though by this time I was such an old hand at the game that I indulged my creative talent by changing the designs—and nobody noticed!

Help-wanted columns constituted most of my serious reading as the weather grew colder. I remember one promising bid for a young girl bookkeeper. Since I had helped my father with accounts in his general store in Placentia I felt well qualified for the job, so I tramped up to the Riverside Drive address. (I always walked when possible to save that nickel carfare.)

A rather handsome middle-aged man answered the bell and escorted me with remarkable cordiality into a den saying I was just the type he was looking for, etc. etc. But it certainly wasn't for bookkeeping. I may be small, but a Newfoundland girlhood in a fishing village had taught me how to take care of myself; and take care of myself I did, to Mr. Lothario's chagrin.

Men were appearing on street corners selling apples, and I noticed that the help wanted columns got very short indeed. But all the headlines in the papers assured me that the depression could go no lower. Being out of a job and broke was no novelty to me. I had moved to a Henry Street rooming house in Brooklyn and used to go down the street to a little restaurant a block away. It was very cheap. Some evenings I would buy a bunch of daffodils instead of dinner, and spend what was left after the 25 cents for the flowers on a big breakfast. But on one particular day I resolutely passed by the florist.

The place served lots of good food at a good price—an excellent idea, I have always thought, for a restaurant. Getting hungrier by the minute, I hurried down the last block, past the Presbyterian church, to arrive at a darkened front and a locked door. A glance at my watch convinced me that it was long before closing time and I banged impatiently on the door. There was no answer. Someone might have died in the family, of course, but I could think of no other place where my 45 cents could be stretched into a decent meal, so after a short wait I knocked again, quietly but insistently.

After some time a light went on and tired footsteps approached the door.

"Oh, it's you," said the proprietor who, incidentally, owned my rooming house. "Sorry, no dinner being served. The place is out of business."

"But you've got such good food. And it's so reasonable here. What's happened?"

"Come in, little Miss Murphy," said Mr. Anthony, "and have a cup of coffee, anyway."

So I had a cup of coffee and heard the sad tale of a small business going on the rocks, even though it was apparently successful. Mr. Anthony pleased his customers and they returned time after time, but his breaking point was so low that his creditors (the butcher, the baker, the linen service people and the landlord) moved in on him before he could get enough diners to make a profit.

"It seemed so nice," he said, "to have a little business of my own—to be independent. But it's hard times and I couldn't charge enough. Now I'll just clean up and get a job as a waiter someplace. I'm a good waiter."

There had been two other proprietors of the little tea room before Mr. Anthony took it over briefly. The first one, he told me, failed for the very good reason that the food was terrible, greasy and unappetizing. He wasn't sure about his immediate predecessor, but I was. He had one of those personalities that would make people turn right around in the entrance and look for another place to eat.

While I was finishing the cup of coffee, my mind was racing madly, but I controlled myself outwardly and asked Mr. Anthony how much rent he paid.

"Twenty-five a week," he answered, "payable in advance, of course."

"Of course. Who's the landlord?"

"Miss Murphy, whatever are you thinking about?" he said, knowing what my questions were leading to. "Don't you get mixed up in this business. It just won't pay off, no matter how hard you work. And besides, this place's got a hex on it."

Hex or no hex, I was talking to the landlord an hour later. The wildness of my plan and my Irish ancestry must have made me very eloquent. After the owner had outlined all the problems facing a young and inexperienced girl in taking over a tea room which had failed three times in a year, he shook his head, and my hand, and said, "Good luck." Knowing I'd need it, I made a deal to pay at the end of the week.

My first move was into the building itself from my furnished room down the street. I wanted to be close to my base of operations. It wasn't as good a room, I recall, but there was a tub in the living room, which meant I didn't have to wait my turn for baths in the community bathroom. Then, feverishly, I started planning.

I had calculated that if I could serve a hundred meals a day with a dime profit on each meal, it would bring me a profit of seventy dollars a week, which would cover the rent and more besides. I immediately started planning menus and found myself giggling over the funny American names of entrees and desserts, such as Swiss steak (why Swiss?) or apple Brown Betty (why Betty? and why brown?) or prune whip. (Was the whip made of prunes or were the poor prunes whipped?)

Next I went to all the stores in the neighborhood, putting myself in the role of a housewife planning a family meal. I was determined to undersell her in her own home, and with wholesale buying I knew I could do it. Biscuits, hot rolls, these were items people didn't bother with often in their own kitchen

—better still, popovers! Nice decorations would be imperative.

Suddenly I realized I'd need help. Off I went to my Columbia University haunts to find a bus boy who could cook and college youngsters who would help out just to get meals at half price. One night I thought to myself: "I haven't even got a name for the place." I was just going to sleep and I tried to visualize my little restaurant—Patricia Murphy's elegant little restaurant with beautiful decorations, delicious food, soft lights—Patricia Murphy's Candlelight, I said out loud. And that's what it was called. (Actually, I used candles because the electric lights hung nakedly from the ceiling.)

The opening day was so frightening that no one in the theatre, the concert hall, or anywhere could possibly have undergone the agonies I did in getting ready for my gala premiere. My student-cooks-bus boys-waitresses were all in the kitchen preparing the fine dinner and finishing up the hand-painted menus. I went up to my room and dressed in my shabby best, for at last, tiny as I was, I was going to be a hostess. In the middle of dressing I had a horrible thought and raced downstairs in a dressing gown. I'd forgotten to set the tables!

But Mr. Anthony, my landlord, who lived on the block, had not forgotten. There he was, arranging each dish and piece of cutlery immaculately and folding the napkins in the pure Italian style. I could have cried from relief. I've always folded my napkins that way in every restaurant I've run.

There was absolutely nothing more to be done except to remember to juggle twenty cups and saucers around so that they would serve for thirty-six setups. I adjusted my hair in the little mirror over the dresser and went out to the stairs. I heard guests at the door. I almost panicked. And then I knelt down on the stairs and prayed.

Chapter Three

CANDLELIGHT AND POPOVERS

My prayers were answered on that hectic opening night of Patricia Murphy's Candlelight Restaurant, but I've always been glad that I asked for very little. All that I wished for was to break a little better than even, so that there could be a second night. Even in my wildest imaginings I did not foresee the success my restaurant business was to become from its humble beginnings in half a basement. Anyway, my kids and I were too busy to think about the future. Customers kept coming and coming. The thirty-six seatings were changed more than twice over to accommodate eighty-four honored and treasured guests, and twenty cups and saucers were properly juggled to see that everyone had coffee or tea promptly. Fortunately, I had ordered enough food. It was good. And the popovers were a great success.

There was a happy bustle about this opening—something dramatic about the evening's routine, even when poor Susan lost a twenty-dollar bill. I had rigged up shelves under the stairs leading down to the little candle-lit room. Cigarettes, candy and inexpensive little gifts were on display, giving people a chance to browse briefly before or after the 65-cent or 85-cent dinner (higher prices, incidentally, than my predecessor had charged). The funny thing is that at that time I didn't really appreciate the high compliments paid me by more than one departing customer who would exclaim:

"The atmosphere is so wonderful, Miss Murphy!" With my realistic fishing village background I imagined they were talking about the weather!

As we couldn't afford a cash register, the receipts were stashed away in a box hidden under a gay display of pots, pans and colorful china. These were arranged in a store showcase which my ice man, Victor, bought for me down on Fulton Street for $3, payable a week later. He brought it in with the ice. We arranged it artistically, even to putting icing around the pans, to make them look like cakes. Several children yelled for pieces of the lovely-looking confections. Fortunately, their parents didn't try to cut into the tin.

During those first weeks of January, 1930, I never thought of balancing receipts and expenditures. As long as people kept coming for the dinners and a 45-cent lunch and I netted even a dime on a meal, I knew I was in business. I paid cash for everything and kept right on doing it until 1950. It didn't hurt my credit. I remember chasing after the ice cream man for half a block to pay him his bill. I couldn't catch him and it was just as well. It was for $29, and I didn't quite have that much after ten days in business. One day a couple of girls from Newfoundland broke the glass on the showcase-cash register. I laughed it off, but it was a terrible blow. I didn't have enough money to replace it.

There were rough moments in those first days. The linen supply service was a racket which gave me shabby goods and service. So I blithely changed it, only to be confronted by a plug-ugly telling me to use his service or else. I chased him out the door with a broom. I suppose I was too insignificant a client for him to carry out threats of reprisals.

I also had delicate public relations problems with some of my customers. Ladies living in the residential hotels of the district had a habit of slipping a lot of rolls and even popovers into their purses and coat pockets, undoubtedly to supplement a pick-up meal in their rooms. When asked politely what they were doing, they invariably said they were taking them to feed the pigeons. It happened that I was saving on butter by spreading apple butter from bowls on the breads before serving. So I would remark, still politely: "I didn't know pigeons liked apple butter."

So much of my business success has been due to instinct, and to such intangibles as hard work and painstaking attention to details, that I still can't quite understand the early, almost phenomenal success of the first Candlelight.

Because the Depression was in full swing, a very important factor in this success was my daily shopping at neighborhood stores, where I could match the prices people paid for lunches and dinners at home. Then I had hot breads, and a sort of party spirit which pleased both large groups and lonely, individual diners, who really felt they were guests. And most important, our customers could order us around, a luxury they couldn't indulge in at home.

After the opening, I had planned to throw a little party for my college friends. We were all so dead tired that we did very little celebrating. Hard work doesn't always pay off, of course, but it gives one a certain accumulation of deserved confidence. Many's the time I've told myself: "Pat, if you could earn a living in Brooklyn during the Depression, you can earn it anywhere!"

There was very little social life for me during this early period; very little, for that matter, until years later when I married Captain Kiernan. There were several attractive boys living in rooms above mine in the Henry Street house. After trying unsuccessfully to get me to go out with them they would knock on my door occasionally and ask, "Pat, do you think you're ever going to amount to anything?"

Whatever I answered, I did think so. Every waking moment I was planning for my little business. A lot of moments when I should have been relaxing or sleeping, I taught my college friends to hand-color menus for the Candlelight and distribute them to people living in nearby hotels such as the St. George, often with little gifts of cookies. Once people came to the Candlelight I knew they'd return. Often I'd stare at passers-by on Henry Street until they must have wondered whether I was "all there." I was only trying to figure out how I could make customers out of them.

One thing that worked well was a bulletin board. The Candlelight was tucked between two churches. Copying from them, I put up a sign case just like those on which the churches announced sermons and preachers, except that mine had menus on both sides. I vividly remember carrying those menus under my coat in terrible weather and slipping them into the frames. Eventually we had a light trained on our "services" and lots of people stopped, read and dined at the Candlelight.

A good friend of mine has called me a "loner," and I guess that's what I am at heart. I had fun with the kids who worked for me, but they got married and moved away. I never even thought of a home life. My restaurant was my home. Here I lived, did my housekeeping and planning of meals, and, quite literally, entertained. If it is possible to make your business your life, I came very close to doing so. For a time I didn't even consider what had happened to my investment of $60. When I had drawn it out of the savings bank to start the Patricia Murphy enterprises I was down to bedrock.

A good friend of mine at the time was Harry Weston, who became a very successful architect and is now practicing in upstate New York. He gave me valuable advice and a pair of very helpful hands during the first weeks of the Candlelight. He even took turns with the kids in the kitchen and did what he could to make our cramped quarters look architecturally interesting and functional. It's surprising what one can do with a basement, a staircase, and even exposed hot water pipes.

It was Harry who came to me as the first month of the Candlelight ended.

"How are you doing, Pat?"

Surprised at the question, I told him everything seemed to be all right; we were still in business and we owed no bills.

"But where do you stand, Pat, after your first month in business?"

Quite honestly, I told him that I didn't have the remotest idea. It had been a day-to-day scramble for me. The idea of keeping books hadn't even entered my head.

"Look, my dear," said Harry patiently, "you add up the money you have in the bank, or in cash, and subtract this week's rent and immediate food and service bills. Then you'll know how much you've made."

I couldn't believe that bookkeeping could be as simple as this, but I was willing to give it a try, particularly since I knew there was no higher mathematics involved. There was a consultation of my savings book, a lot of jotting down of figures and a peek into the Candlelight's hidden "cash register." After a little figuring I burst out:

"Harry, look! I've made $500."

He smiled indulgently, dusted off his dishpan-reddened hands and said tersely, "Pat, you'd better hire a dishwasher."

I hired a dishwasher immediately—for $12 a week (a seven-day week), in case people have forgotten what labor costs were in 1930. But it took me some time to realize fully what had happened to my little restaurant. Sixty dollars had become $500 in four weeks and in the worst depression this country was ever to experience! It seemed incredible, but there were the figures! My simple make-do formulas had proved not only practical, but astonishingly successful.

Fortunately I took stock at that very early period in my career. What had diners-out in Brooklyn, during hard times, been given that brought them back to the Candlelight in increasing numbers and netted it a handsome profit, I asked myself. They were charged almost nothing for overhead, and nothing for my services; they were given lots of good food at prices that compared favorably to the cost of meals cooked at home; they were treated like favored guests in something of a party atmosphere; and there were no glum faces to remind them of their problems.

After Repeal and my first liquor license we had a *real* Candlelight party—with wine, something I had not been able to serve in the restaurant. We really celebrated, and Harry Weston made a lovely toast to our continued success.

From then on we had a bowl of daiquiris, all mixed, on the hall table to cheer incoming guests. The bowl was borrowed from the Presbyterian minister next door. As he handed it to me with a big smile, he said, "Don't let the ladies know about it, Miss Murphy."

It wasn't all clear sailing after that, I can tell you. Even when you treated them like special guests people could be very nasty. They knew they could order us around, and some of them did so when there was absolutely no need for sharp commands. Some people just love to criticize. I remember one spinster lady, a teacher with a doctor's degree, as a matter of fact, who liked the food and prices well enough to dine at the Candlelight four or five times a week. After we had been open for a few months, though, I overheard her talking to a waitress. She was saying, "Is she still putting water in the mashed potatoes instead of milk?"

I marched right over to her, but then she was all smiles and greeted me like a long-lost friend. It was silly of me to take remarks about the restaurant personally, but I was young and I worked so hard to make things pleasant and felt so personally involved in the business that I had some very unhappy moments. I would even cross the street to avoid passing customers who had been rude to my nice waitresses or had said mean things about the food.

A very pleasant episode at this period started out in a rather frightening way. I had gone up to the subway entrance next to the St. George Hotel to see my friend Benny, who is now quite a figure in the garment trade. He was a news dealer and he was awfully nice about letting me have change (I was still having trouble in this department.) He waved me back frantically from behind his kiosk at one end of the damp, cold subway corridor, and pointed toward the turnstile. There I saw a gaunt, frightened German shepherd dog racing around in terror and scaring the daylights out of the subway passengers. I didn't hesitate, but walked up to the poor animal and sat down next to him on the cold concrete while I petted and soothed him. He liked me from the start and gradually stopped shivering and whimpering.

Then I was in a fix. What was I to do with the puppy? I knew my landlady would never permit me to bring him into my small room with the bathtub at one end. I decided on subterfuge. I knew her telephone was in the back of the house, so I called her from the corner pay booth and then hung up, getting my nickel back. While she was struggling to find out who was calling her, I sneaked up the front steps and into my room with my new pet. She wasn't very bright. I did this for days.

I called my new-found friend Flukey and he was a wonderful dog, although I don't think his pedigree was of the best. Before long everyone adored him and he had his own entrance to the back yard, down the fire escape. I had Flukey for many years, and have rarely been as grief-stricken as I was when I had to have him put away after he had become very old and ill. My other Brooklyn pet was a duck I called Dora. Much to my horror she turned out to be a cannibal. Her favorite food was scraps of Long Island duckling, which the diners fed her with glee.

As the Candlelight became too small for the customers I had to expand, so I broke through into the basement of the adjoining brownstone and took over the back yard. Jack Lynas, a painter and interior decorator, helped me with the decorating of the enlarged quarters. We painted trees on the walls and constructed a lovely fountain in the back yard. Later we put a terrace along the parlor floor and the seating capacity more than doubled.

No one will ever know what a garden meant to me. The painted trees were all very well and created a pleasant background, but I cherished a real live ailanthus tree which came with the back yard. It was a problem tree, for it attracted caterpillars; but I *had* a touch of garden. To think it took me twenty years to have a real garden of my own!

People still twit me today about the struggles I went through to get more customers in the Candlelight. They remind me that I took the fountain out and planted a couple of tables in its place. This was not done entirely to get more patrons. It happened that the Methodist minister from the church next door considered himself a charter member of the restaurant. (At his request he was always given a finger bowl, little knowing that it was merely one of the glasses in which we baked deep-dish apple pie.) He complained about the fountain and "the dull monotony of falling water." This made me mad but, after all, by removing it I got a larger turnover.

The Depression, as you may remember, became a lot worse before the country's economy slowly recovered. My little business thrived for a time until I was netting $50 a day. I always counted by the day then. But businesses were failing right and left and competition became murderous in the restaurant field. From my small beginning efforts at luring in hotel residents, I had worked up a brisk mail circulation of my menus. However, two of the hotels thought I was cutting into their coffee shop business, and threw my announcements away before they reached the guests. One of the hotel clerks who distributed our announcements, and got some fine free dinners in return, was fired; but I got him another job quickly. And I got my Candlelight menus spread around.

This was helped by a bunch of enterprising youngsters who actually pretended they were visiting guests at the various hotels in the neighborhood. I had little aprons made which fitted under their coats and had pockets in which to carry the large numbers of hand-colored menus. They would go to a particular floor and then walk up and down, slipping the news of good food at fair prices under doors. One of my "undercover agents" ran into trouble in a neighboring hostelry. She didn't know that alternate floors in this hotel were assigned to men and women. When she asked the elevator operator to let her out on a floor dedicated exclusively to males, she had to do some pretty fast and glib talking to the house detective. You can bet I never let her go back *there* again.

One nearby hotel in particular went into direct competition with the Candlelight with great success, teaching me early in my career not to count on customers' loyalty. They instituted a dinner for about the same price that I was charging, but they offered a shrimp or oyster cocktail for only 10 cents extra. The Candlelight had a shrimp cocktail for 15 cents extra. We wouldn't handle oysters with our tiny kitchen. You would scarcely believe it, but that confounded 10-cent-extra shrimp or oyster cocktail almost put me out of business. Even our best customers left us. They would go by our little two-sided church-announcement bulletin board looking kind of shamefaced. Some would even cross the street. But pass us by they did, and it was agony watching them leave us. In a few days we were serving sixty-five people a night instead of 350—fewer diners than we had had at our opening!

People have asked me so many times what drove me during those tough first years of struggle, struggle, struggle. It wasn't a dedication to the restaurant business. It certainly wasn't the intention of making a fortune. I guess it was the sheer urgency of necessity—mother of all invention.

Shortly after the opening of the Candlelight, I heard from one of my father's friends that the fishing industry in my home town of Placentia near St. John's had been virtually wiped out by an underwater earthquake. Being the kind of man he was, my father, Captain Frank Murphy, didn't let me know about this. For nearly two years he kept his general store open, supplying fishermen and their families on credit. He felt responsible for them. They were his friends and neighbors as well as his customers and he looked after them as long as he could.

But suddenly I became the chief family breadwinner. I brought my mother to Brooklyn for lengthy visits and then for good. My sister Sheila, the baby of the family, helped out briefly at the Candlelight, until I sent her to Packer Collegiate Institute and Wellesley College to study.

You cannot do this sort of thing with a few thin dimes for profit. I worked harder than ever, spending hours at the old Wallabout Market, where I got fine food at very good prices and where they gave me great bunches of celery or lettuce, taking pity on the harassed small girl who, some of the stall-keepers thought, might be collecting for Sisters of Charity. My meat came from one of the finest wholesale butchers in town and I never skimped on quality. The bar was a great help because it kept people happy while waiting for tables. In the summertime, when it was really hot, I had a big punch bowl in the little garden with a big cake of ice floating in the fruit drink and a pretty girl to pour it, free of course, to waiting customers.

I worked Saturdays, Sundays, holidays and late evenings. This was partly because I was a sort of frustrated housekeeper. I never had a home of my own to keep. Also, I worked when I really didn't have to because the boys and girls I hired were working these hours, and I could darn well do it too.

Urgency was the only possible reason for this sort of endless labor, endless planning and scheming to make dining at the Candlelight more attractive and thereby get a greater turnover of customers. And, of course, it paid off. For I weathered the whole bleak stretch of the Depression, even expanding a bit. By 1938 I was looking for new fields to conquer.

I often wonder what would have happened had I drawn the $60 from the savings bank and gone back to Newfoundland at the start of 1930 instead of gambling it all on the Candlelight. It would not have been a very promising future, what with my father about to go out of business because of the wholesale destruction of fish.

But I have always cherished pleasant memories of a happy girlhood in Newfoundland. It was a unique background for a career woman—wild and primitive, and yet for me filled with a vast sense of security, and the chance to learn early the simple fundamentals of business. So I shall digress from my little enterprise in Brooklyn and return to a small fishing village in the far North.

Chapter Four

NEWFOUNDLAND GIRLHOOD

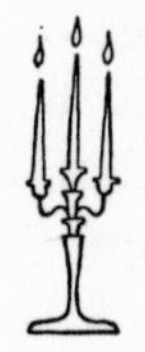

These things I remember most vividly from my childhood: my father's wonderful general store in Placentia where "everything from a needle to an anchor" was sold . . . the crunch of heavily packed snow underfoot (a very cold crunch peculiar to Newfoundland) . . . being boosted into a freight car in the dead dark of early morning to lay a wreath from the convent on the bishop's coffin . . . a disreputable fortune-teller who read small girls' fortunes in tea leaves and predicted I should have a fine house with two chimneys (I didn't believe her, but Kinsale fits the prophecy) . . . an ice cream parlor in St. John's called the Blue Puttee which had lovely little cakes. . . .

But let me begin at the beginning. I was born in a small Newfoundland fishing village, Placentia, not far from St. John's. It was a town of curious contradictions; it had a tradition of its own and figured historically in the struggle between the French and English to dominate the peninsula, but was, in reality, a frontier outpost.

There were almost no automobiles, even in the 20's. And the way to keep meat during the winter was to hang a whole frozen steer outside the door and chop off roasts, steaks and chops as needed. These were supplemented by caribou, rabbits and partridge. It was wild and primitive, but it held great enchantment for a curious young girl.

My family had the first telephone in the community. My father, Frank Murphy, was the leading Merchant and citizen of Placentia, sharing high honors, of course, with the Priest, the Doctor and the Magistrate. His big general store was the focus of daily living for the fishermen, the trappers, and their families. The store lived up to its motto: "Everything from a needle to an anchor," and Captain Frank was known up and down the Newfoundland coast, and all the way south to Boston, U.S.A.

My most vivid recollections of girlhood center mainly around the store, where I busied myself whenever I was permitted—keeping accounts, taking inventory, selling, and engaging in all the sideline activities that went with a barter system.

My father also published a newspaper, with "Murphy's Good Things" on the masthead. It carried all sorts of personal notes, marriages, births and—most important—obituaries. When my hair was still down my back I was interviewing relatives of the deceased and making up the most important-sounding death notices I could concoct. I'd pore over the dictionary, finding the biggest possible words to describe our people. My father used to chide me gently for some of my write-ups.

What I liked best, though, was selling in the store. This I started, as I remember, after I had gone off to St. Michael's Convent in St. George's to study. As soon as I got back for vacation in the winter or summer, I would hurry down to the store out on the wharf and beg to be given every job at hand. It required quite a knowledge of the inventory and the prices, for I actually did sell needles and anchors and every conceivable article in between. Working on the four-page paper, "Murphy's Good Things," helped, because all new items from foreign ports like Cadiz, or from St. John's, were advertised. I quickly learned the business and even helped my father with the accounts, although I was never any great shakes in mathematics. To this day I can't really figure in terms of much over a hundred dollars, although I can "count the house" and not miss by much.

At the convent I got a conventional education and the chance to read prodigiously. Much of the reading had to be done surreptitiously, with a flashlight hidden under the blanket at night, or in unoccupied rooms at odd hours during the day. I read all of Dickens and most of the other 19th Century classics. Of course, I could never talk about the books at school, so I had to wait for vacation. My father approved of this habit, even though the good sisters frowned on it, and I always went back to school loaded with volumes from his bookshelves.

One day I had slipped away from the other girls during the recreation period and was happily ensconced in a deserted pantry looking at the pictures in a dog-eared society magazine. The clothes fascinated me, as did the backgrounds of great houses and busy streets—all so strange to a little girl from Placentia. Then I heard someone coming to the door. I hurriedly hid the magazine under my uniform blouse, holding both arms awkwardly against it to prevent it from slipping. In came a new young priest from Ireland (now Bishop O'Reilly) whom I had only seen once or twice at the convent. We stood facing each other for what seemed hours, and then he asked me if I wasn't going to greet him. I tried something resembling a curtsy and he burst out laughing, saying:

"You'll do better, girl, if you take that magazine out from under your blouse."

I pulled it out, scared and mortified, but I had to know what was going to happen.

"Are you going to tell on me, Father?"

He smiled indulgently and shook his head. I have always liked him.

The sisters were not all so understanding, although as I look back now, I see that I was really spoiled by them. For one thing, I was the youngest girl in the school. And for another, my father, Captain Frank, was a great and close friend of Bishop Power, having gone to school with him. With all the devious cunning of a small girl, I built up a Damon and Pythias relationship between the two and never failed to allude to it when I was in danger of severe punishment. Only one sister was my enemy, or so I thought—a big Irish woman. One day I was standing next to her in the choir. When the sermon was over, she said to no one in particular, in a tone of quiet resignation, "A big head and nothing in it."

I could hardly wait to tell the other girls, and when I did we all went into paroxysms of giggles. Unfortunately, the young priest overheard me, and this time he did tell on me. I was uppity and didn't mind punishment, but I wasn't prepared for what happened. Sister descended on me in a towering rage, but instead of dealing out the routine punishment she satisfied herself with two words. "Bad girl!" she fairly shouted at me in front of all the girls. She couldn't have punished me worse. To be called a "bad girl" was the most humiliating thing I could think of at the time.

But on the whole I fitted rather well into the routine of St. Michael's and had a happy and profitable schooling there. One of my favorite nuns was Sister Xavier, who taught both music and housekeeping. I was far better at the piano than at "neatening up." I'll never forget being told to sweep the stairs one day. I had never had this chore before. I started in on the first step at a great rate, but when I was half through Sister Xavier quietly said:

"Patricia, it's better to start at the top when sweeping stairs. You can just keep moving the dust on down and they'll be clean when you get through."

Mother Superior Acquin (you see, I still remember the names

of almost all the people I knew in Newfoundland) was another lovely woman. She had come over from Ireland where she had been raised as a great lady before taking her vows, and I could never hear enough from her of the fine brick houses, the bustling towns, the elegant carriages, and such delicacies as mushrooms, which I could only imagine, never having seen one. It used to make me very sad to see her at dinner, where great platters of eggs would be set down at the sisters' table. She had what they now call an allergy to eggs, but she would sit there smiling with her bread and tea as eggshells were cracking all around her. It has always seemed to me that people's sensitivities about food should be paid very careful attention. I would have had the eggs covered up at the very least.

Mother Aquin (short for Aquinas) loved flowers, and it was she and my mother, Nana, who gave me my first love of exquisite blossoms and of growing things which serve no practical purpose. If I'm not mistaken, it was Mother Superior who lent me the magazine I was caught reading in the pantry. I do remember that it had some wonderful pictures of English and Irish gardens. When I was finally able to devote some time to flowers and to raising orchids, I brought Mother Acquin the first orchid ever seen at the convent. I sent her other flowers regularly until her death.

There is one death that I remember in every slightest detail to this day. When good Bishop Power, the former schoolmate of my father, died, his body was sent to St. George's in a freight car. It was mid-winter and I was awakened by the nuns hours before dawn and led down to the railroad siding. The snow crunched ominously that black night and the lanterns lent a fitful light to the procession of dark-robed sisters and all the pupils, including a small girl. They had contrived a wreath out of house plants and ground pine; when we got to the freight car they handed it to me, perhaps because the bishop was a friend of the family or because I was the youngest girl in the convent.

I remember being boosted, rigid with fear, through the sliding doors of the car. A raised lantern showed me the coffin set on two-by-fours, and then there was no light at all. Shaking with cold and terror I forced myself across the few feet of rough boarding and thrust out the wreath, almost throwing it on the coffin. I stumbled back to the door. When the nuns lifted me down to the snow I burst into uncontrollable sobs. It took the sisters some time to soothe me for what they thought was simply grief over the bishop's passing.

It was in that same winter that it took me twenty-one days to get home for the Christmas holidays—winter can be very severe in Newfoundland. But at the age of twelve, I didn't mind at all. I remember learning to play cassino on the train, and at one stop of several days at a small town the train crew taught me how to snowshoe. We explored the village and the woods around it, and I became quite good at pushing the clumsy basket-feet across the crust. We ate rabbit stew with dumplings and toasted marshmallows and sardines. Physical hardship, desolate wastes, even being alone, were things I grew up with, things I accepted as a matter of course. It was a tough training, but it stood me in good stead when I had to fend for myself and survive in a grueling and hazardous occupation. Many years ago people talked about the virtues of a log cabin background on the American frontier. My own beginnings were not very different.

Earlier I mentioned the frozen sides of beef which people who had cattle to slaughter hung in the back yard for meat during the long winter. But I remember far more vividly eating game of all sorts: venison roasts, steaks and stew, partridge, rabbit, caribou, wild geese and ducks. Chicken was a rarity and eggs came from partially-tamed wild fowl. We didn't know what turkey was, but fish always filled in menus—salt salmon and codfish, never codfish cakes, which must have been eaten exclusively in Boston. Many people, mind you, had no such variety of food as the Murphys. They weathered the winters with salt fish and brewis (which was simply hardtack), fat back, seal flippers, dried peas, and beans and molasses.

The salt fish and brewis came from our general store, as did the rabbits, which constituted an important item in bartering, being exchangeable for cloth, sweetening, tea and the like. I remember a very mean woman who came to the store for a rabbit one day. Two of the boys saw her coming and cut a hole in a rabbit's foot, filling it full of air with a bicycle pump. She was delighted with such a fat delicacy, snatched it up before someone else could get it, and rushed home. She was back soon, complaining bitterly to my father, "It was blew, it was blew." When she described the fat rabbit she had made away with, Captain Frank gravely said:

"We never have fine rabbits like that in the store."

This same woman had a predatory goat which had the bad judgment to descend on my mother's little flower garden one day. This was no ordinary garden, but one which it had taken courage, imagination, dedication and toil to bring to flower. The base was rock slabs, and even as a small girl I remember gather-ring seaweed and anything else that might turn to soil to make ground for seeds. But Nana's green thumb, which I seem to have inherited, resulted in a profusion of blossoms.

It was these that the tactless goat had started to munch when Nana descended in high dudgeon, with a permanent cure for the animal's depredations. She had soaked a bit of old mop in tar. The foolish goat grabbed it hungrily. That was the last we saw of him.

It was Nana who told me the great story of the Murphys' coming to Newfoundland:

"Your great-grandfather, Pat, was a proud man, and he didn't like the English. He was a great patriot in the region north of Dublin and well-known. After a bit of trouble when some soldiers were shot, he made his way, travelling in the dark of night, to a big port and boarded a ship bound for Newfoundland.

"The captain said he had no room for him. I think probably he was afraid to have him aboard. So up steps a young man by the name of Keating, gives him his papers and says:

"'I'll go ashore. Nobody will know me. But if you leave the ship, you'll be shot.'

"Your great-grandfather actually arrived here as Keating, but he took his own name back and acquired a big tract of land which was known locally as Murphy's Plantation. Nobody knows what happened to Keating."

Nana was always a tower of strength and has remained very close to me through the years. It was she who encouraged me in my music and in my busying myself about Captain Frank Murphy's big store.

I loved the store and often think I would have loved being a merchant—not that I don't do quite a bit of merchandising in my gift shops in Westchester and Fort Lauderdale, where the turnover amounts to some hundreds of thousands of dollars annually. One of my greatest delights today is to travel and find lovely things, from sugar plums in Lisbon to fine Irish linen and jewelry, for my customers. For when I was a girl, the fishing ships coming back from abroad were so keenly awaited by all of us. Having sold their cargoes of fish, the boats were loaded with treasure for their return trips: rum, wine, molasses, dried fruits, salt, grapes and Valencia oranges. The whole town would turn out when a boat came in with its goods from foreign parts. My grandmother had a shawl all the way from Paris, and a brown bonnet with dark red trimming.

Fishing was the chief occupation of the town, and took the men out to the famous Newfoundland Banks for long periods. They were ingenious about maintaining a balanced diet. Vinegar warded off the scurvy, but they would also take vegetables and other greens and cover them with rendered fat—a primitive form of deep freeze. No one ever knew how they kept bread from molding for months. All I know is that they hung it from the beams of the fishing boats.

The chief problem was the winter months when parts of the bay would freeze solid. Then the men would cut lumber—"pit props" we called them—drag them down to the river and secure them by roping the outside logs together. Once I remember, vandals cut the ropes on a large consignment that was to have been floated out to a freighter anchored off Castle Hill Fort and bound for Cardiff, Wales, and the coal mines—a long way from Newfoundland. The men were afraid to handle the pit props. My father persuaded the freighter's skipper to let him bring the ship through the narrow passage to the wharf under Murphy's Store, against which the logs had drifted. The whole town cheered as he moored the freighter and the logs were saved. I remember we had a big party at our house for the ship's officers. I was sixteen. We had a dance and the second mate tried to kiss me. I wouldn't let him.

A far greater exploit of Captain Frank's, to my mind, had an audience of only one. Funerals, as I've already mentioned, were very important in Placentia. When they were being arranged, the families of the deceased never used the front door of the store; after signalling my father, they would come in by a side entrance and in decent privacy pick out linings for rough-hewn coffins or material to make burial clothes. There was a soft nun's cloth which was a favorite, but one tough fisherman said it would never do for his dead wife.

"Her backside would be out of it in two weeks," he said.

But when Bridie died her family was not even able to get to the store, since they lived across the "gut," and it was one of those breaking-up times of late winter when that strip of water was unnavigable because of clampets—great chunks of floating ice. There was no need of a dress for the laying-out, but white shoes were a desperate necessity. Captain Frank was informed by telegraph. He rummaged through the storeroom and found a pair of white shoes that would fit Bridie. Then he set off for the gut with me tagging along.

It was bitterly cold, but I was filled with a glow of excitement and admiration as I watched my father leap from clampet to clampet across the gut to deliver the white shoes. On his return the ice had shifted and he had to take a wider part of the estuary to make the crossing. He was glad to be back, and whirled me off the ground in a great bear hug.

One of my proudest moments was when the first typewriter was delivered in Placentia. I set it up in a corner of the store out on the pier, but with my back to the window (I've never been able to work with a view at hand). Suddenly I was conscious of someone looking through the window. Sure enough, there was old Pat, whom some people called the village idiot, peering at me intently. He meant no harm but was fascinated by the machine that wrote words.

"Ye're a great hand at it, aren't ye," he said, and went away.

Actually I wasn't too good at it; nor could I master the old-fashioned printing press on which "Murphy's Good Things" was turned out. But I well remember an American publisher by the name of Monroe arriving in Placentia one summer for fishing. He saw the typesetting outfit, laid aside his rod and reel, and spent his whole vacation making up our newspaper.

All this time I was working very hard at my music and developed a conventional classical piano repertoire. Once a year an examiner would come to Newfoundland from Trinity Music College in London, and he was surprised to find a musical youngster in Placentia. He was very stern. On one occasion, when I was playing a Beethoven sonata, he stopped me sharply in the middle of a passage.

"You're playing that wrong," he barked.

I started over, phrasing it exactly the same way and before

he could interrupt I turned to him and said, "I think I'm playing it right."

The teachers and pupils in the hall were horrified and expected the examiner to flunk me out of hand. Instead, he nodded his head gravely and told me to finish the sonata. I got the top mark in the district.

It seems strange, as I look back, that it was music which led me to New York and success in a very different field. Of home economics I learned absolutely nothing during my youth. I was always being shooed out of the kitchen, for I had fancy notions about food and used to improvise recipes that as likely as not would turn out for the worst in the cooking. There were no restaurants in Placentia to inspire me as a caterer or hostess, and those in St. John's were nothing to boast about, although I do remember the little shop with the singular name derived from the First World War, the Blue Puttee. It served delicious cakes and cookies and it was nicely, if simply, decorated. It had a sort of party atmosphere, which I've always tried to have in my own restaurants.

Sometimes, in looking back, I feel that this was another life, another existence. But from fishing village to Brooklyn Heights and Manhattan's East Side there was a continuity in my basic outlook, in my quest, even in my restless striving.

Chapter Five

ON SIXTIETH STREET

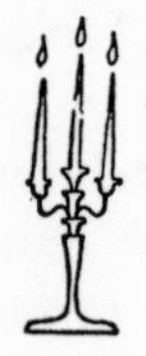

Anyone who has been the breadwinner for a large family will know that the situation makes for a fierce and continuing urgency. Candlelight and popovers had brought me some success in Brooklyn Heights. Considering my minute initial investment of $60, the continuing bad times of the Depression in the 30's and the hazards of the restaurant business, I might have taken considerable pride in the fact that in 1939 my elementary bookkeeping showed a tidy profit of $50 a day.

But I could see no chances for future development and expansion in the staid Borough of Churches. True, I had obtained a liquor license a few months after Repeal, and the good rectors and parishioners of the two churches that elbowed the Candlelight had no objections to my clientele and their drinking habits. It was a big day when the Candlelight served a 20-cent martini. Wine, as I remember, was the favorite beverage in the mid-thirties and was priced correspondingly low. Actually, there was little profit from my tiny bar, though it served the purpose of keeping waiting diners happy. Food has always been my specialty. But while customers crowded the Candlelight for the moderately priced luncheons and dinners, I knew for sure that I couldn't raise prices, and we were as close to capacity business as it's possible to get in the restaurant trade.

So I had to look for new fields to conquer. I could scarcely have made it harder for myself. Partly because many of my experiences in Brooklyn had been so rigorous, and partly because of the vast challenge of Manhattan, I made straight for what I thought was going to be the new center of doings in New York—Park Avenue and 57th Street. A new building had been erected there with a fine spot for a restaurant such as a second Candlelight, catering largely to hotel dwellers in a residential area. Someone arranged an introduction to the landlord's agent, and I marched in prepared to do business, elevating my five feet as far as I could with high heels.

Would you believe it—I was greeted with frankly unrestrained laughter. The agent patiently explained that my letter of introduction had announced me as Pat Murphy and he had thought I was a man! So I wasn't a man, I told him, hardly keeping my temper, but I still wanted to lease his restaurant facility.

"I don't think you quite understand the problems," he said, still amused at the sight of a small excitable young woman trying to break into the competitive arena of Park Avenue and 57th Street. This was just not done. He didn't have to spell it out. Aside from being young and tiny, I was blackballed in advance by my sex. I may have controlled my fury at this particular interview, but the fact that women are discriminated against has always made me mad, and I've championed scores of girls and women who were looking for careers ever since that time.

It was through my friend Jack Lynas, who had decorated the walls of my Brooklyn Heights Candlelight with trees and installed a lovely fountain in a dreary back yard, that I found a way to bring candlelight to Manhattan. He had heard of Betty

Barclay's tea room on 60th Street, just east of Madison, and took me around to see it. He had a talent for visualizing attractive surroundings which has since made him an accomplished muralist and interior decorator. I wasn't in the market for any fancy decor, but I liked the place and the location. It certainly was challenging for a young woman who had started on a shoestring in a Brooklyn basement.

Betty Barclay was one of those ladies whom you would expect to find running a tea room. She liked serving luncheon and would have as many as eighty at midday; then she would take the afternoon off and return around five for dinners for perhaps sixty people. Of course her prices were considerably different from what I had been charging at my Brooklyn Heights Candlelight. And when she told me that an ambitious and energetic proprietor might possibly do a $300-a-day business I was sold. It took an awful lot of people at 65 cents and 85 cents a head to make anything like that in Brooklyn.

Manhattan was very new and terrifying to me. There was an entirely different clientele with entirely different tastes and different ideas of what constituted good values in the way of food. A new set of employes greeted little Patricia Murphy with vast scepticism, convinced that I couldn't make the grade in this rather high-toned district. And then there were machines, big stoves, refrigerators and the like which scared me. They always have, except when my husband, who was a naval architect, ran them for me during the years of our marriage. To give you an idea of how nervous I was about my new undertaking, I got Betty Barclay's permission to go on using her name during the first months on 60th Street.

Also I concentrated even harder on keeping Brooklyn Heights a thriving enterprise, and continued to make my home there. This, of course, required a constant shuttling which I've been stuck with ever since. No sooner had I solved the various problems that were always presenting themselves in my original restaurant than I had to switch my thinking and planning, and myself, to 60th Street. This was not conducive to rest, or to something which was merely a word to me—vacation.

I guess you might say I had half a vacation my first summer on 60th Street. What with popovers, flowers, and the "atmosphere" I no longer mistook for the weather, the new Candlelight prospered from the start. The customers at Betty Barclay's tea room doubled in almost no time; I leased the premises next door before the hot weather came. I had been told emphatically by my predecessor that there was no point staying open in July in this particular part of Manhattan, but with the Candlelight business booming the way it did right into the spring, I didn't believe her. Summer closing is just a silly tradition, I thought, or a chance to take a vacation. So at the end of June I smiled smugly to myself as over 150 people came to the Candlelight for lunch, and many more than that for dinner. Came July 1 (it's still hard for me to believe it) and the luncheon trade dropped below sixty. I bucked the July hoodoo for a couple of weeks, but business grew worse and I finally closed up, giving my Filipino boys vacations with pay—a rather remarkable departure in the restaurant business at that time. They were fine employees; I wanted them back and I wanted them happy.

This was when I had half a vacation. The Brooklyn Heights Candlelight never closed in the summer. I guess Brooklynites weren't accustomed to taking the midsummer off the way residents of midtown Manhattan were. Then, too, my customers in Brooklyn knew they would be comfortable, for I was one of the first restaurant proprietors to install air conditioning, 'way back in the early 30's—1932 to be exact. The York Ice Company let me have a unit practically at cost, although $1,400 seemed like a fortune to me at that time. Then we worked out an arrangement for company salesmen to bring prospective customers in for a sort of free demonstration of the newfangled device. Let me tell you though, I got lots of criticism for my pioneering efforts. Old ladies assured me that their rheumatism came directly from my efforts to make the Candlelight comfortable in sweltering hot weather. When I introduced frozen vegetables, the same patrons were horrified; I had to have the frozen foods secretly delivered.

In any case, I had no money for air conditioning that first summer on 60th Street, so I closed. But instead of taking a rest I used to haunt Mr. Cerutti's small restaurant across the street, and watch people stop and then pass by the closed Candlelight. Mr. Cerutti was very sympathetic. One day he counted forty-odd people who might have been customers had we been open and urged me to make another try, but I had other schemes. If I had to miss midsummer business, I decided, I'd more than make it up after the heat waves. My friend, Jack Lynas, went to work on the premises next door and we toiled like slaves to get it ready for the Candlelight reopening.

In my enlarged 60th Street Candlelight I dressed up any old furniture I could lay my hands on. Against one wall I placed a large mirror and then built shelves against it and covered them with blooms. It created "atmosphere" and people were able to preen themselves in the glass between the flowers. Actually, I was merely "making do."

Two big changes occured in my whole approach to business during the early period on 60th Street. I introduced lamb chops as a regular item on the menu, something I never would have dreamed of doing in Brooklyn, and I encouraged the patronage of white collar working girls, who were just becoming a factor in restaurant luncheon trade.

In the first case I had some tricky ordering to do. My lamb chop special was priced at 75 cents, which may seem ridiculously cheap if you do not remember the period, but would have horrified my Brooklyn customers as incredibly expensive.

I waited in an agony of apprehension to see if anyone would

order the chops. Far from being shocked at the price, a lot of patrons came in especially for this one-time standard American luncheon dish. As it turned out, I never ordered enough lamb chops, and one of my Filipino boys, Jo-Jo, had the frantic task every midday of rushing off to one of the high-priced Madison Avenue butchers to get additional chops. After he had left, more and more people would pick the tasty special and I'd be calling two or three times doubling and tripling the order. Of course, this was "making do" until I learned the different tastes of Manhattan lunchers.

As for the secretaries and salesgirls who started patronizing 60th Street, I couldn't have been more delighted to see them, both from a practical standpoint, as they constituted a huge new group of restaurant goers, and because of my deep feeling of kinship for them. You can imagine my indignation when some of the matrons and dowagers who lived in nearby hotels came to me and objected strenuously to my allowing "riff-raff" to patronize the premises.

It wasn't easy, running two establishments as far apart as my two Candlelights. It took a heap of travelling. Almost at the start, I bought a blue roadster with a rumble seat—second hand, of course. I remember it cost $750. I would do most of my ordering in Manhattan and weigh everything in the 60th Street kitchen, for there have always been ways of cheating customers in the food business. Then I would apportion enough groceries to last 60th Street through lunch and dinner, greet early arrivals, and head for Brooklyn in my blue chariot. After stocking the original Candlelight and seeing that there were no immediate problems, I would drive back to Manhattan and care for late luncheon guests while preparing for dinner. Jo-Jo was always ready to supplement our larder. Frequently I would make trips back and forth twice a day. Once I was right in front of the Wanamaker's store when a man hailed me, not to ask me what I was doing with a rumble seat bulging with food, but to offer me $1,300 for my treasured roadster. I'm a good business woman and I appreciated the tidy profit involved, but I had a feeling about that blue bus and turned him down flat. Besides, the war was imminent and cars were getting hard to come by.

The summer I almost had a vacation turned out to be one of the busiest I can remember. In order to secure the premises next door, I had to relocate an artist and his ballet dancer friend. I've looked for apartments for myself, but I never went through such a frantic and frustrating job as I did for this couple. I'd find something just right and there would be objections. I tramped the streets and finally found them a lovely garden apartment in Greenwich Village. It's hard to believe that apartment hunting could play such an important role in running a restaurant. The other relocation job concerned an employment agency in one of the East 60th Street buildings, of which I now had three. There is an old New York statute that forbids the sale of alcoholic beverages in a house where an employment agency is quartered. I finally managed to obtain a liquor license several years after opening on 60th Street. As I have said before, food and "atmosphere" have been my specialties. I remember well that my total receipts the first day the bar opened amounted to only $20.20. It got much better, but I always considered the bar a place to make people linger until they could be seated, rather than a place to drink a lot. From the outset, I wanted to see a lot of people waiting to be served, and today, like a theatrical impresario, I am delighted when lines start to form at my restaurants.

The lines formed when we opened the enlarged Candlelight on 60th Street. I'll never forget the day before the opening. My Filipino boys were wonderful, running about, frantically getting ready for the big moment. After it was all over we had a huge celebration feast. I remember a wild variety of things going into pots of melted grease, all of it heavily laced with onions and garlic. Then I beat a hasty retreat—the first and last I have ever had to make from one of my kitchens.

The food they prepared for a whole new set of luncheon and dinner guests was something else again. The prices were still reasonable. People in this part of town were eating out more and more, and the Candlelight flourished.

Even so I was terrified that I wouldn't be able to make both ends meet. Once a month I had a payment of $800 to make on my premises. I would arrange to meet the owner's wife around 3 o'clock, and then check on my bank balance. I knew that by waiting until bank closing time, I had a day of grace. I was still in the elementary stage of bookkeeping.

I used to stand at the door of the Candlelight to greet people. The new room couldn't be seen from the street, and potential diners would glance in, see people waiting for friends to join them, and decide to turn away. I would step firmly in front of them and assure them that there was lots of room in the back. Talk about pulling people in off the street!

It wasn't until the bar opened that I knew the Manhattan enterprise was a success. Even though the first day's receipts were so small, the little alcove where drinks were served gave a convivial note to the Candlelight and made people less impatient about waiting their turn at table. One incident about the bar opening caused quite a flurry. There's an old superstition that your first customer at a bar must be of the Jewish faith. At the last moment I rushed across the street to a florist I knew named Eddie Cantor, grabbed him by the arm and rushed him into the Candlelight.

"How do you like it?" I asked, pointing at the small alcove.

"Fine, I guess," he announced, out of breath and somewhat bewildered.

"Well, you've got to have a Manhattan."

He didn't want a Manhattan. In fact, he didn't drink, certainly not in the middle of the day. But finally, still bewildered, he took a proffered Manhattan and I could relax again. I've always been thankful for my Eddie Cantor, the florist from Goldfarb's.

The people I had been leasing from were Christian Scientists, and they frowned at the idea of drinks being served on their property. So when I got my liquor license I bought them out. Knowing I was able to guarantee $105,000 for the title lessened that awful feeling of urgency, particularly as I was able to make arrangements without the help of bankers. As recently as twenty years ago, they still looked askance at a young woman in business.

When friends heard that I owned the 60th Street Candlelight, they couldn't believe it at first.

"Pat, you're the darndest," they said. "We remember in Brooklyn Heights when you were happy to make a thin dime on a meal. Think of all the thin dimes that have rattled into your cash register to make this possible."

"No time to celebrate!" I said. "We've work to do."

And work we did, roofing over the back yard of 60th Street and finding room for sixty more customers at the Candlelight.

As I look back on 60th Street, I see that this is when I really crashed the big city. I had made a go of it in Brooklyn, against heavy odds, but Sixtieth Street gave a different glow of candlelight, brighter and more exciting. It was through my second Candlelight that I finally met the man who was to give me my happiest years.

Chapter Six

MORE CANDLELIGHT ON SIXTIETH STREET

As I look back on the 60th Street Candlelight it meant not only crashing the big city but also making a success of a somewhat un-wished-for career. I had succeeded in Brooklyn, amassing a working capital out of the "thin dimes" Jack Lynas referred to, but it wasn't the big time in any sense of the phrase. Potatoes even more than popovers were in top demand in the provincial district of Brooklyn Heights, and there's not too much you can do with potatoes.

Moreover, there was very little personal satisfaction to be derived from the ferocious amount of work and constant rebuffs. Many times I thought of trying other businesses. As a matter of fact I have, even going as far afield as the import and export cotton trade. Perhaps I would have made a clean break with restaurants if it hadn't been for 60th Street. Many women tend to go from one thing to another, but I stuck with it once I had invaded midtown Manhattan.

While still confined to the Brooklyn Candlelight I became

involved in a curious sideline, once again prompted by that ever-present inner urgency. Father and his fishermen customers in Newfoundland were up against it after an underwater quake had ruined the cod fishing. I thought I could help them out by importing lobsters for the New York market. I had tanks built on coastal freighters to keep them alive, but I was really a greenhorn—I didn't know that lobsters eat each other, and I didn't know that fish dealers eat each other too. They wouldn't handle my lobsters at the Fulton Fish Market; when I took them off the boats myself, in a truck, I was so held up that I had too few live lobsters to market.

But I'm pretty stubborn. I got a concession in Canarsie to run a cafeteria for the Brooklyn Union Gas Company. This was truly a "thin dime" project, since the restaurant was supposed to furnish a hot meal for twenty-five cents. Anyway I had an outlet for my lobsters, and I imagine that for a brief interval I ran the only metropolitan eating place in history that had fresh lobster on a twenty-five-cent table d'hôte lunch. The diners liked the lobsters, but they had plenty of complaints, as in any company cafeteria. We had a suggestion box, and one of the demands made was for larger water rolls instead of bread. Also among the objections was one I had encountered in my first Candlelight: the gas company employees would have no frozen vegetables. Fresh vegetables or else.

With those awful lobsters still driving me, I made one final attempt to market them at Jones Beach. I'd take them to the Brooklyn Candlelight and cook them, then dash out to a stand at the beach. I remember using an old punch bowl belonging to my grandmother as a showcase. Into it went the biggest and reddest lobster of the lot. The others were dished up in a variety of ways. But this operation was too much. I knew when I was licked and I gave up the lobster importing business.

One source of income that proved very helpful when I was planning my invasion of Manhattan was catering. I could prepare luncheons at the Candlelight and serve them in Brooklyn schools. This also gave me a bit more flexibility in planning my menus in the restaurant. I did very well for a time serving breakfasts at a riding academy. This extra money I could put back into the business or save for my expansion to 60th Street. I always made money, thank goodness. I served people what they wanted at good prices. And I worked like a stevedore.

The experience in dealing in the wholesale market, running concessions, and catering was immensely valuable. More important perhaps was the wide variety of people I ran into during these side excursions. People tell me that I have an instinct for satisfying the tastes of diners—their tastes for pleasant surroundings and gracious service, as well as for food. An instinct such as this may rest in part on a God-given talent, but most of it, I think, comes from tough discipline and trial-and-error learning. Anyway I learned, I prospered, I got a terrific amount of discipline and I didn't make too many errors.

But what a relief it was to really start making a big go of it on 60th Street. There were less than 200 seats, but before long each of them was occupied two or three times at a meal. However, I never stayed open Sundays as I did in Brooklyn.

I paid my bills every day as I had at the start. Pots, pans and dishes were all bought by me—at bargain prices where possible—and every penny was personally accounted for. It meant much more work, but there are not many short cuts when you are trying to satisfy hundreds of people daily. A competitor who was doing some comparative shopping in the Candlelight was appalled to find out that all the tomatoes I served were peeled.

An equipment salesman was equally startled to find out that I made all my coffee in individual pots. (The simple truth was that I didn't trust myself to make really good coffee in an urn.) He had all sorts of ideas for streamlining the Candlelight.

"You know, if you took my advice, Miss Murphy," he said, "You could serve 500 people here a day."

"I'm doing it now," I replied. He flipped!

One thing I did add was a salad bar. It proved extremely popular, particularly in the spring and summer months.

When I had acquired three buildings on 60th Street, I knew that my new Candlelight was glowing brightly. Even this physical expansion was done the hard way. I'm reasonably certain I could have gone to a bank and financed the purchase of the two adjacent houses (one of them the old Meehan home, which had quite a history), but I was the original cash-and-carry girl and I was still mighty defensive about my sex. I remembered well that original turn-down I'd received on 57th Street when the agent discovered that Pat Murphy was actually a "miss."

So I went to the cash register regularly and made my payments, hoping that the increased profits would stand the strain of expansion. Actually, there was no need for worrying, which I can assure you I did regularly. One of my new buildings had a back yard, and I followed the trend of the times and instituted outdoor dining for a very brief period. We put in a fountain; it was very European and relaxed, I suppose, but it didn't solve the problem of winning new customers and a constant turnover. Out went the fountain and the al fresco dining. The yard was roofed over and a lot more tables were installed.

All this excitement was not without its headaches. I was still commuting madly between Brooklyn and Manhattan, frequently carrying the provisions in my blue roadster, and caring for every detail of the two restaurants personally. I no longer had to have Jo-Jo rush to the local butcher for eight lamb chops, but I did have to create tempting new dishes to keep my diners happy. Many of these have been Candlelight stand-bys ever since. (You will find recipes for some of them in Part III of this volume.)

The thing that terrified me most about the restaurant business, as I've already mentioned, was machinery—principally the possibility that it might start acting up. And my greatest fear of all was fire. In spite of all the precautions I took and the fact that my staff knew about my phobia, we had a small blaze in the kitchen one day at lunch time. One of those oven gas jets started acting like a Roman candle.

My reactions were instantaneous and, I suspect, very feminine. One of my oldest employees, who was a sort of kitchen manager, rushed upstairs to tell me the kitchen was on fire. All I can remember was sliding down those iron steps leading to the basement, taking one look around and calling the Fire Department. They responded very quickly, but not before I had completely recovered my composure. When the first fire truck arrived I was on hand to direct it and succeeding engines to the drug store down the block. From there men and hoses were escorted through a back entrance to the kitchen, and the Candlelight lost no luncheon customers.

That was fine until I discovered that my brave smoke-eaters had turned off the gas at the emergency feed-in. It was Saturday afternoon. I called the gas company, which refused to turn the gas back on until Monday. I can't remember all the details, but here again the feminine touch must have been in evidence. A couple of firemen returned to the Candlelight, surveyed the situation, and by Saturday dinner the gas was working again and we served a capacity crowd.

I had one other experience with the Fire Department, but the oddest part about *this* crisis was that there was no fire—no fire at all.

I have always leaned over backwards to insure the best sanitation conditions, so I was delighted when cans of compressed insecticide were first placed on the market. One day—it was a Saturday again, I remember—I had some British cousins visiting New York. It was shortly after England declared war on Germany; they were training flyers in Canada for the R.C.A.F. I don't particularly like night clubs and girl shows, but I knew that these young aviators would, so I had arranged to take them down the street to the Copacabana. Before this small gala, though, I had to try out my new insect bombs.

I started spraying the basement, after seeing that the food was all properly protected. At $4.95 a bomb I realized that it was going to be quite expensive unless I moved fast, so I tore around spraying walls, floors and ceilings, then quickly dressed and took my cousins to the night club.

While we were watching the high kicks of the chorus girls, a curious passer-by saw smoke coming out of the Candlelight basement and rushed to a fire alarm box. This time the engines stopped right in front of the restaurant and men with picks started smashing in windows. One of our cooks saved the day before I was notified. I had rented a room for him in an adjacent building. When he saw the commotion in the street and men with axes attacking the Candlelight, he flung himself between them and the restaurant with outstretched arms.

I found him there, holding the Fire Department at bay. When the firemen discovered that the smoke was only clouds of insect spray they left rather sheepishly, but I was soon visited by the head of the Fire Department himself.

"Look, Miss Murphy," he said, "I appreciate your dislike for insects. But next time you go crazy with spraying, do it late at night; and, just to be on the safe side, better call us up and tell us what you're doing."

My cousins, incidentally, said they had never had so much fun nightclubbing.

There were minor and sometimes amusing tribulations. But with the approach of the war things became very difficult. Anyone in the restaurant business will tell you that the confusion and red tape that came with the setting up of the O.P.A. and rationing could scarcely have been worse. At times one was penalized for honest mistakes. Then there were the constant offers from the black market of opportunities to secure provisions underhandedly. It took courage as well as honesty to keep a level head during those years. I had to close the original Brooklyn Candlelight at lunch time for the duration of the war, but 60th Street stayed open.

That restaurant was a favorite, I am happy to say, of servicemen from all the Allied nations. We had a small mantel in the front entrance on which soldiers and sailors put their caps when they arrived for lunch or dinner. They didn't have to take their turn in waiting lines, either, but were seated as soon as they arrived if there were any vacant places. One time, I remember, a big bearded sailor and his companions were standing somewhat impatiently in the lobby-bar. Suddenly I remembered a corner upstairs where I could squeeze in an extra table. "Come on upstairs with me, boys," I said cheerily—and in my innocence missed the knowing glances that followed this invitation. They practically bounded up the stairs after me. When I had led them to the secluded alcove, the big fellow with the beard turned to me expectantly:

"Aren't you going to take off your hat?" he asked.

Since the Brooklyn opening I had been looking after my family, sending them what money I could, and bringing my stalwart mother down from Newfoundland for visits. Now I was able to maintain her and my baby sister, Sheila, in a Brooklyn apartment, and take care of my sister's schooling.

It would be pleasant to note that my new affluence gave me a chance for pleasant, leisurely living after the years of downright drudgery; but this wasn't the case. In my youth and inexperience I married an equally young and irresponsible man, who was himself a Wall Street broker. I took a lovely little town house in the East Eighties and tried my hand very briefly as hostess of my own home, but the relationship was doomed from the start. I moved to Brooklyn after I realized this, and the marriage was terminated with an annulment. Nana was a tower of strength during this unhappy interlude. Before the annulment was granted, in spite of her religion, she urged me to get a Reno divorce.

There is one thing that can be said for hard and even back-breaking work. It is a wonderful refuge when one is faced with personal unhappiness. In this first, sad romance there was not enough affection, understanding, or companionship even to lend the dignity of tragedy to my memories. Still, I counted it a failure on my part as well as anyone else's. And I am only grateful that it ended quickly and that I had my Candlelight to guide me into the future. I was so occupied that I had none of that dangerous surfeit of idle hours in which I might have brooded over my bad fortune or withdrawn from the world of everyday living.

Chapter Seven

ENTER CAPTAIN KIERNAN

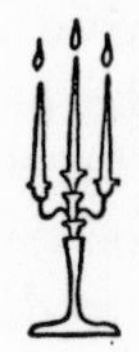

There was no blinding light or clash of cymbals when Patricia Murphy and Captain James Kiernan met. But there was a lot of snow. The most snow, I believe, that New York has had in modern times. It was the end of December, 1947, and the last thing in my mind was meeting a handsome stranger who was going to sweep me off my feet. It would have been very easy to miss meeting him or even seeing him a second time. I missed the first time; he missed the second; but we came together just the same. Perhaps it was foreordained and inevitable. All I know is that once we came together we stayed together.

He was to have been my escort, my "blind date," I suppose you might say, at a party friends were giving me at the Lotus Club on New Year's Eve. All I had been told was that I would meet a distinguished naval architect. And then it snowed. And it snowed! Parked cars were covered in a blanket of white. Traffic was practically paralyzed. Very few people ventured out at all. Like so many things in my life, this big snow was a personal challenge to me. Here I was, a native of Placentia, way up north in Newfoundland where winters were really winters. Who was I to be dismayed by a few feet of snow in New York? I determined to keep my two Candlelights open no matter how bad the blizzard.

Fortunately, I was well stocked in the 60th Street restaurant, but I had to get supplies to Brooklyn Heights by evening. Trucks couldn't move so I hired a fellow with a light station wagon, who made it with the groceries as far as the foot of the Brooklyn Bridge, where he got hopelessly stuck. Still undaunted, I got out of the station wagon and rounded up a bunch of youngsters with sleds. We made a game of mushing through to the Candlelight, where they all celebrated the adventure together. My friends at the Lotus Club started telephoning me, but a party was the last thing I had in mind with the challenge of the blizzard to meet. I begged off.

Instead I made it to the subway, went to 60th Street to say a Happy New Year to all my employees there and returned to the Brooklyn Candlelight to celebrate with my original staff. The fact that there were virtually no customers in either restaurant didn't bother me, although part of my desire to keep open in spite of the elements was prompted by the old urgency of keeping in business each day, making enough to pay the bills, which I was still figuring on a daily basis. It's strange how compulsive business can be, particularly when one is in it alone and against great odds. I may not have made much money in the big snow, but I kept open.

By this time I had quite forgotten the Lotus Club Party. I went back to Cloverleaf, my little house on Cranberry Street, and took my cocker spaniel, Sir, for a floundering walk through the snowdrifts. When I got home the phone was ringing. My friends begged me to take the subway to Manhattan and join the party, which was still going strong. I told a real whopper.

"I'm afraid of the crowds in the subway on a terrible night like this, all alone," I said.

My friends were not to be put off so easily; they assured me that they were not afraid of the subway and were coming to Brooklyn to see me.

"There's nothing to eat in the house," I said rather plaintively, but they had eaten and they were on their way. They had to use the kitchen entrance. The snow had quite covered the front door.

I'm not sure when I first noticed the handsome Navy Captain with the ruddy complexion. I think it was when we both took some bottles of champagne out to my little garden and tucked them into snow banks to chill. He was helpful; I approved. But I took no further notice of him until one of my friends started talking about the annual dinner party I gave each January at the Plaza. The man in uniform looked sort of left out of things, so on an impulse I said, "Would you care to join us for dinner, Captain Kiernan?"

"I'm sorry," he answered, "I have a previous engagement that evening."

Would you believe it, I was vastly relieved. I'd regretted the invitation almost immediately. I didn't know this man, nice as he appeared to be, and his acceptance would mean getting him a pretty feminine companion. After all, he had been dragooned into the Lotus Club party to escort me. This small complication was over and I was pleased.

But it didn't work out that way. It snowed again, and I had to postpone my party for a few days. Captain Kiernan must have heard this from a friend of mine. I was reading in bed one evening when he called to say blithely that he could attend my dinner at the Plaza after all. I was quite taken aback, but assured him that I was delighted.

Here was another challenge. I was stuck with this Navy character. I had to get him a date for the dinner. So I decided to arrange for the prettiest girl around. And I did. She was the daughter of a celebrated Brooklyn doctor, a model, and a genuine beauty.

So I saw him a second time at the Plaza, where my party was a great success. His date was ravishing, so I paid him practically no attention during the evening, feeling that he was well taken care of. Instead of hustling the beauty off at a reasonable hour, though, as I expected, he stayed and stayed until he was virtually the last guest. His excuse was reasonable. It was snowing again and even the taxi drivers were quitting, particularly when a prospect asked to be driven to Brooklyn, where the model lived.

So I became the good Samaritan. I had a car for the occasion, and I told him I would taxi him and his date to her apartment. Once there, Captain Kiernan made a pretty but very brief good night speech to his lovely companion and promptly rejoined me. We drove to the Cloverleaf, but instead of giving me the conventional thank-you farewell he asked if he might come in for a nightcap. He did.

Promptly at nine the next morning he was on the phone. I thought he had lost something at the party, but instead he wanted me to go to dinner with him that evening. This seemed pretty fast work to me. I told him I had my two Candlelights to look after and that it was out of the question. He was not to be put off.

"I'll drive you back and forth," he said. "That way we can see something of each other."

What could I say? He tagged along with me on my chores, and from that night on I saw him every single day until we were married. Our excursions were rather prosaic. Rosie, the nickname he won for his ruddy complexion, didn't like the theater; in fact he didn't care for any of the rather sophisticated activities I had engaged in since really discovering Manhattan. He took me to hockey games, prize fights, ice shows and an occasional operetta. He was a good dancer, but a knee injury during the war made it difficult for him, so we generally skipped the supper clubs.

We talked a great deal. He found out all about the girl from a Newfoundland fishing village. I discovered that he had graduated third in his class at Annapolis. He had been the youngest graduate in the history of Annapolis, although he'd waited a year to enter because of his extreme youth. After a brilliant career as a naval architect, and an authority on the dreadnaught, he had been assigned to Admiral Nimitz's staff at the start of World War II. Then he had been sent to Germany before the breakthrough, to build bridges over the Rhine. He worked on many of the ships we constructed at home and abroad. For a period after the war he was stationed in the Philippines, where he installed such hygienic measures in Manila as watered streets, an unheard-of thing to the natives, who preferred to wait until it rained to get rid of germ-laden refuse.

These snatches of his background were not volunteered, any more than the fact that his father had owned a yacht. I had to pump him unmercifully, and it took years before I put together the main outline of his career. But whether we talked about ourselves or merely the weather we seemed to be together each day, and to be quite satisfied about this arrangement.

One thing was certain, right at the start. He was the handiest man I had ever known. The somewhat elaborate kitchen equipment always terrified me, but Rosie had a sort of communion with machines, and he was always there to fix things, just as he had been ready to help me ice the champagne on our first meeting. It was a strange sort of "going steady," but go steady we did.

And then he got quite reckless and asked me to go to the opera. It was the night of February 13th. I raced out and bought a lovely gown. I dressed to the nines and got out my finest jewelry. If I do say it, I was quite a contrast to the little girl in a sailor hat with streamers down the back who had decided that 14th Street basements couldn't possibly be representative of the New York she had dreamed about. I should have been more superstitious about this first big date of ours. Imagine, on the thirteenth!

It snowed, of course, and it turned very cold. Rosie telephoned and suggested that we had better go to the Metropolitan Opera House by subway, as taxis would be hard to come by in such a blizzard. I was furious, for I couldn't figure out what I could wear for both the subway and a box at the opera; but I changed into something or other. Realizing that a restaurant was out of the question, I cooked a fine dinner for him with the help of Nana, who was living with me at the time. I had just about resigned myself to discarding my finery when the doorbell rang and there was Rosie, all bundled up against the whirling snow and wearing bright blue ear muffs!

"What in the world are you wearing those horrible-looking ear muffs for?" I blurted out.

"It's bitter cold out," he answered serenely.

"But you can't go to the opera in ear muffs."

"Oh, yes I can," he said with a big smile.

We went and the opera was fine, although I've completely forgotten the performance. In the intermission we went to the lounge and had a couple of Coca-Colas served by a disdainful waiter. We were very gay and we felt in an ear muff mood. On the way back to the box he pulled me around and kissed me lightly on the forehead. It startled me. Believe it or not, up to that moment he had not even held my hand.

Then he leaned over and whispered in my ear.

"You know what I'd like?"

"I'm not sure. No, I don't know."

"I'd like you to be my wife."

When we got home that night Nana knew at once, and she was terribly happy for us. The strange thing is that from the moment he kissed me so chastely during the opera intermission we two, who were always talking—even interrupting each other—didn't say another word for the rest of the evening.

Rosie didn't like the theater, as I've said, but I insisted on his taking me to "Mister Roberts," which was a big hit, with Henry Fonda in the starring role. I had arranged a party, with George K. Arthur and his wife among the couples. After considerable grumbling my beau said he'd go, and even dress for the occasion. During the first act I was startled when an elderly woman reached over and grasped Rosie's arm, saying: "Thank you, General, for saving my son."

Then in the intermission people stared at us so hard that I was afraid my slip was showing. In Shubert Alley, Lee Shubert came up and told Rosie he was glad that he was attending the show.

Later Rosie told me what this was all about. It seems that he was an uncanny look-alike for General Eisenhower (trust his sweetheart never to have noticed this). When he was on the Western Front, before the crossing of the Rhine, some officer from Intelligence came to him and asked him if he'd consider a rather strange assignment. Since he was a dead ringer for the Commander-in-Chief of Allied Forces, they suggested that he dress exactly like Eisenhower, with the general's stars and medals, and move from place to place behind the lines, convincing spies that Eisenhower was leading the offensive from spots obviously quite remote from his headquarters. He politely declined, but the more he thought of the idea the madder he got, and he finally declared himself with a good many unprintable words thrown in.

"It's a crazy scheme and wouldn't fool even the dumbest blank German. And why should I set myself up as a decoy for a blank prowling assassin? If I'm going to be shot, I'm going to be shot with my own good name and in my own good Navy uniform and not in a blank army issue."

He lived in Brooklyn and even with my busy rushing around and the shuttling back and forth, we found ourselves together a great deal, particularly in the evenings. I can't remember one evening I missed seeing him between the first of the year and July 12th, when we were married.

I forgot to mention, in connection with Rosie's first kiss, the shy signalizing of our engagement. We were at the Sonja Henie ice show some days after the wonderful opera-going in a blizzard. We were enjoying it hugely and at one point, when the line of skaters swing way out on the ice and then whip around to make a circle I didn't think they were going to make it and clutched Rosie's arm. To my surprise he put his hand over mine and before I could withdraw it he took off his Annapolis class ring and slipped it on my third finger, the only one that it would conceivably fit. Again, we did not speak to each other for a long time.

Rosie had very simple tastes and he appreciated my restaurant operations, for I was serving good food at very modest prices. Since we often dined at the Candlelight, he thought that all eating places were similar, I guess, but he had a rude awakening one evening. I was determined to get away from business and I wanted something entirely different, so I coaxed him into taking me to a very swank restaurant in the East 50's. He couldn't understand how I could dream of eating out. When he found we'd have to wait in line for a table, he had his excuse for marching out of the place.

But there was a small French restaurant across the street and I steered him into it and persuaded him to order Boeuf Bourgogne, which I knew was a specialty of the house. He had it and liked it, as I remember, but when he got the check he went through the ceiling.

"Do you know what they charged me for that Boeuf Bourgogne, Pat?" he said in a loud voice, much to my embarrassment. "Four dollars and fifty cents, Pat. Four dollars and fifty cents for pot roast!"

Prices of things were always astonishing to him. Partly, I suppose, it was due to his long career in the Navy where there is a considerable difference between cost to servicemen and those to civilians. Actually, his feeling for elementary values was close to mine, which gave us something solidly in common.

We prospered nightly in Brooklyn and on 60th Street. Rosie had become an ideal partner in my Candlelight career. He looked after the machinery. He took over annoying personnel problems and gave me time to think up ways of making my places more attractive.

Most important, he let me blow off steam. When something had gone badly wrong I would fix things up quietly, controlling my anger beautifully, no matter what stupidity or negligence had been involved. Then I'd rush in on poor Rosie in private, pouring out my woes and indignation on him! He understood this perfectly. He would calmly listen to my storms of complaints and protests, let me get them out of my system and then give me wonderful advice or assume the problem himself. This sort of attitude makes for a great partner, and an even greater husband.

With the coming of 1950, we were doing so well that Rosie said, "Pat, you've got to get a break. You've been working like a dog since you first went into this business. What you need is to get away from it all. I'm going to get you a country house and you're going to devote yourself to a life of leisure for a change."

"Where's the country house going to be?" I asked, not at all sure that I was ready for even semi-retirement.

"I've found a wonderful spot."

But it never was a country house. It became my third Candlelight Restaurant.

Chapter Eight

MANHASSET CANDLELIGHT

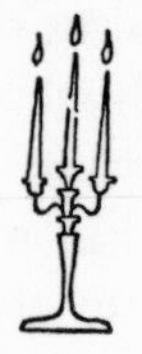

When rosie first suggested getting a country place, I was pleased at his thoughtfulness, but my chief reaction was purely practical. Shaking my head, I simply queried, "When would I ever stay in it, dear?"

"All right," he answered. "Let's have a country restaurant then. Maybe you won't work so hard when you're surrounded by trees and flowers."

I gave up gracefully. And none of us—and I mean Rosie, the help, and everyone connected with the project—ever worked so hard in all our lives as we did in Manhasset.

At least we didn't have to start on a shoestring. We had six months to prepare for an opening and consider the problems of running a suburban Candlelight, with all the differences in clientele, tastes, and accommodations that this would mean. After considerable scouting, Rosie and I found a suitable place in Manhasset and started remodelling it. As a concession to Rosie, I even agreed to rent a small cottage nearby where I was supposedly to take time off from the project to rest. That, I assure you, I was never able to do in Manhasset.

Once more I was involved in a trial-and-error undertaking, with hundreds of thousands of potential diners as my target. I knew next to nothing about Long Island and its inhabitants. What was more worrisome at the time was how to attract hordes of automobiles from miles around to one small spot where there was a congenial restaurant.

I had discovered even back in the early days of the Brooklyn Candlelight, and certainly on 60th Street, that more and more people were eating in the country, particularly on week-ends. By a good guess I anticipated the huge exodus to the suburbs that was under way. And by instinct, I suppose, I figured out a few fundamental things that would make people happy dining in the great outdoors.

For some reason parking had always been concealed at rural restaurants, with cars sneaking around behind the establishments to park in most inconvenient spots. I established my parking lots right in front of the Candlelight, reducing the trouble for car drivers. Then, with an eye to keeping people from leaving when the restaurant was crowded, which I hoped would be most of the time, I started attractive planting arrangements all around the Candlelight. In fact, I launched rather furiously into the art and science of horticulture. You will find some of my tips to flower lovers in Part II of this book.

Even this was not done without upsetting incidents. Well do I remember a couple of 60th Street matrons who ventured out to Long Island to view "Patricia Murphy's Folly." One slapped her gloves contemptuously at a beautiful planting of rare rhododendrons I had flanking the entrance walk. She turned to her companion and said:

"Think of her being able to pick her own flowers!"

Far more upsetting was the flood. I'd never realized that Long Island was so low. The rains came, puddles formed and there was no place for the water to go. Finally Rosie, who was something of a mechanical genius, got some fire hose and a pump and rigged them up at the entrance to the Candlelight, where we had erected all sorts of improvised bridges to let the customers get in. Some water experts arrived and said his scheme was against nature, but he persevered and finally drained the entrance. He was like that. Whenever anything went wrong, the cry went up: "Get the Captain."

The only problem I had with him was his desire to save what he considered unnecessary expense. He would put low-watt bulbs in spots where I wanted the brightest illumination. When I started my system of taking reservations at the door and seeing to it that the first who came were the first served, he would have none of pneumatic tubes, but worked out a system of collecting the slips with clothespins which could be lowered on lines.

But he worked tirelessly and without him I would have given up many times.

One of his self-appointed jobs was to take the cash to the bank to deposit in the account of the Candlelight. It seems that he did this meticulously, keeping the bills in their proper places according to their place of issue, and packaging them beautifully. After a few months of this, the president of the bank sent for him and told him he had noticed his meticulous handling of bills.

"How would you like a job here?" he asked.

"I've already got a job," Rosie answered with a smile. "I'm Patricia Murphy's husband."

If nothing else, the Manhasset Candlelight was a good testing ground for ideas in suburban dining which were to come to a fine flowering in the Westchester Candlelight. Floods weren't an everyday event, and Rosie and I had a chance to try out all sorts of schemes. Some of these, to be sure, proved more interesting than practical, but trial and error was as good a method as any for a young woman who had started off with thirty-six seatings and twenty cups on a busy Brooklyn street.

In the process of remodelling we connected a big old house and a garage nearby, making a lot of extra space which was certainly needed after a vastly successful opening. More than anything else, it supplied room for people to wait for tables, particularly when the weather was bad. It was then that I remembered my early job as a cashier, when I had tried to help out by selling candy and cigarettes while making change.

"Let's have a gift shop, Rosie," I said. Perhaps somewhere in the back of my mind was a nostalgic yearning for my girlhood days of selling in my father's Newfoundland general store.

At any rate we started selling all sorts of trinkets and merchandise, including food. Everytime we travelled I would be on the watch constantly for items I thought might appeal to my Manhasset patrons. Moreover, the shopping gave them something to do while waiting.

Lo and behold, the idea caught on from the first. Profits from the gift shop climbed to $40,000 and then $60,000 annually. Suburbanites obviously liked to combine dining out with casual shopping, particularly since they had their own transportation and weren't forced to carry packages through crowds or on public conveyances.

In the interest of atmosphere, I dressed my waiters in bright red jackets and my waitresses in becoming frocks, varied according to seasons and especially decked out for holidays. Many rural restaurants now have brightly costumed personnel, but I believe my Manhasset Candlelight was the first large suburban place to go all out for help that was good-looking and smartly turned out, as well as courteous.

With flowers I made only a small beginning, but it was a start. In addition to the rare rhododendrons flanking the entrance I had successions of blooming plants and shrubs, mostly of the hardy variety, such as roses and begonias; but customers were surprised, and frequently came to the Candlelight to see the surroundings as well as to dine.

One experiment that was tried out and abandoned was a lot of fun while it lasted. I arranged to have an outdoor spring painting show, with a few professional artists to give helpful hints to the amateurs. It was colorful and appealing to my patrons, and they actually turned out some quite creditable canvases on occasion. What mattered to me, with my omnipresent sense of urgency, was that these daubing and drawing festivals made customers turn up by the hundreds. Even on what are known as "slow days" in the restaurant business, my busy would-be artists would rub the paint off their fingers with turpentine and then sit down to relaxing luncheons and dinners.

Rosie and I had no idea what a big success my "country place" would be. Even with numerous extensions and parking in front of the restaurant, there never seemed to be enough of it—particularly in Westchester, where I recently put a Mercedes-Benz lounge car into service to take customers the sometimes considerable distance from where they parked to the Candlelight entrance. At least the lessons of Manhasset made it easier to plan the expansion that later became a recurrent problem.

Of course the greatest joy in Manhasset was having someone dear to me with whom to plan, experiment, and talk over each day's problems when the frantic activity was finally over. Without Rosie I don't think I could have stood the heavy load of running the Manhasset as well as the 60th St. Candlelight and the original Brooklyn Heights Candlelight on Henry Street.

He would always be up before me and would wake me every morning with coffee and vitamins and Royal Queen Bee Jelly, which was quite a fad in the '50s. We would have a little time to plan the day's activities, and then we'd both be so busy that we'd hardly see each other. Occasionally I'd call him on the intercom, just to hear his voice.

Fortunately for both of us, we bought Kinsale—my Florida

home—during this period. It gave us short respites from the fierce, grinding urgency of supervising three utterly different and widely separated restaurants all at the same time. Kinsale was and still is my real home.

Chapter Nine

CAPTAIN KIERNAN AND KINSALE

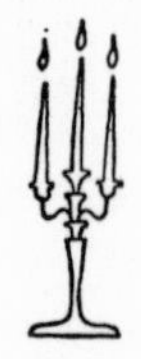

MANHASSET CANDLELIGHT WAS certainly no country retreat in which I could relax, but Rosie was determined that I should have one. Curiously enough, we were very close to it just at the time that we were first struggling on Long Island, but it took three years for it to materialize. In 1949 we spent a portion of the winter at the Jupiter Island Club at Hobe Sound, Florida. We both fell in love with the country, the wild simplicity of it, and kept coming back to a rented cottage for three years running.

We really wanted a country place, but much as we liked Hobe Sound, we didn't want a house there. So for three winter vacations we drove the back-country roads, enchanted by the semi-tropical climate, the natives and the spots so beautifully described by one of my favorite authors, Marjorie Kinnan Rawlings. We looked at big houses and small houses all through the region surrounding Palm Beach. Several times we actually passed what was to become Kinsale, but it seemed big and forbidding and I wouldn't even go up the driveway. It was called "Bel-Air." All of the features which I now love about the place—its random, sprawling contours, its mixture of vegetation, its sheer size—put me off until I was able to fully visualize its complete change-over into Kinsale. The truth was that I really didn't want a big house. We looked at smaller houses but liked none of them. We practically gave up.

Then, for no reason at all, we were driving one day down the road to Bel-Air again. The water looked so inviting that we stopped the car and walked up the driveway. It was boarded up and forbidding, but we saw the lagoon and the island and the creek, and we got the real estate man to show us through the interior. It took us just ten minutes to decide that this was it. Otis, a sort of caretaker, was there with his eight children and I thought: "It will be nice to have Otis on the place."

Rosie and I hadn't exchanged a word but we understood each other so well that we didn't have to discuss our mutual decision. As he walked down the front steps, Rosie turned and said, "Otis, you have a new mistress."

The most astonished person in this whole group was the real estate man. It was very cold at Hobe Sound that winter and Rosie had decided to take me to Key West to get warm. We only had a few hours before leaving, but we stopped in at the tiny real estate office in Stuart, signed the contract and paid a rather large deposit on the place. Then, of course, I started to worry, but I was secretly delighted and my head was whirling with ideas for remodelling and landscaping. This was our home. This was my first true home since I had ventured out of Newfoundland to seek a great musical career in New York. I had made a long journey by candlelight.

We wanted to name it "Cashel." That was the town in Ireland from which Captain Kiernan's mother had come. But there was another lovely old house nearby called Cashel, another big place which I couldn't look at—and very luckily, as I look back on it, because it had far less grounds for my experimental gardening. Then one day we were out in a boat, not far from the front of our house, where the St. Lucie and Indian Rivers meet. We saw the two white chimneys of the house, and Rosie pointed at our island and said, "Look at that headland, Pat. It's just like Kinsale as you sail into Ireland from the West."

So we named our place Kinsale and always said to each other, "There's no sale like Kinsale."

I'm supposed to be a good business woman, but I made some expensive mistakes. We had bought a great deal of acreage and a house that was far too big and expensive for two people, so we sold off a number of parcels to finance the renovating and gardening we wanted to do. Then, as Kinsale started blooming into a showplace, we found people clamoring to build on small lots all around us; so we bought back all our land at twice the price for protection. We had a difficult time getting back the land we had sold along the creek. We had to find a comparable place for the owner of the lot, and that took doing. It reminded me of having to find a garden apartment for a tenant at 60th Street when I was establishing the Candlelight there. Anyway we retrieved our wonderful combination of creek and back-woods, the lagoon with the island beyond, and one of the highest hills on the east coast of Florida—all of twenty-seven feet above sea level!

Unlike my Candlelight restaurants, Kinsale was a place where I could spend as much time planning, or just relaxing, as working and doing. We bought Kinsale in 1951 and it was four years before it was anywhere near the way I wanted it. Even now I am planning ahead. For one thing, I had to learn a lot of new methods of doing things, from guarding against the annual threat of hurricanes to gardening in a region where four crops and three or four bloomings a year are the rule. The wonderful thing about a home that you love, though, is that it is never really finished. It goes on growing more beautiful and more livable and accumulates layer after layer of devoted care. I know that during the sorrow that was later to come to me, it was Kinsale that pulled me through several tragic and shattering years.

Remodelling the house was a big problem. There was hardly a place where one could see our lovely lagoon and island; this meant cutting windows and building patios. The dining room, paradoxically, was both too small and too large, so we put in a bay window and a marble floor. Local workmen were astonished when we used a beautiful native stone, coquina, for the edges of the terraces, rounding them off. Rosie was astonished at the price of lawns. One day he grumbled, "Why couldn't we have just painted the ground green, Pat?"

My biggest thrill, I think, was the chance to be an important hostess on my own at last. I have had as many as 675 guests at a time at Kinsale, with orchestras playing, and it never seemed crowded. With the indirect illumination which Rosie installed behind bushes and rocks, and the orchids and other rare plants which I had growing everywhere, Kinsale was a beautiful setting for parties. St. Patrick's Day was our great "at home," with everything, including the ice, bright green, with swinging of shillelaghs and dancing of jigs. I'll never forget Otis in his first green top hat and green cutaway. In addition to elegant affairs we had an annual "left-over party" at the end of the season, when we cleaned out provisions except for eggs and milk. One year, I remember, we had frogs' legs, which I sautéed with white wine, crème de menthe, beer and a wild assortment of foods from the freezer.

One affair which I dreamed up is, I believe, unique. It was great fun. I called it my "around the clock" party. It started off in the morning with a Victorian breakfast on all the terraces and patios, included an al fresco lunch around the swimming pool and on the lawns (overflowing into the elegant cabana if it was rainy or chilly), and wound up late in the evening with an after-opera supper in front of the Kinsale fireplaces.

Entertaining meant a lot of work, for I supervised all the cooking, tables and decorations, just as I have always done in all my restaurants, but I loved it. It is one thing to entertain and feed people comfortably and contentedly, at a price, in a business establishment, and to make sure that every bit of one's investment of time and money is paying off. It has its own satisfactions, to be sure; and after all, it paid the bills, in my particular case, for the gracious entertaining at Kinsale. But the sheer joy of making people happy and giving them pleasant memories in one's own home is something else again.

On a less expansive scale, I took great delight in putting on garden parties for local groups, and even for tourists passing through Stuart. By diligent trial and error I had succeeded in growing many temperate-zone flowers in the lush Florida climate, and beyond that I always imported typical New York and New England blossoms for these occasions—quince, lilac, forsythia, primroses and laurel. I'll never forget one old codger who came over to a display of primroses. He put out his hand and barely touched them with something approaching awe. His eyes were filled with tears.

"Miss Pat, I haven't seen primroses in years and years. Thank you, Miss Pat."

Being a career Navy man from Annapolis and having lived around the world, Captain Kiernan was more used to the receiving than the giving end of parties, but he was wonderful in helping me out. He particularly loved table settings and would go to infinite care in arranging for, say, a seven-course dinner. Then he loved to arrange costume parties, turning a terrace into an oriental courtyard, or making exotic settings around the cabana and swimming pool, or taking a boyish delight in placing musicians on a balcony or behind shrubbery so that our guests never knew when they would be serenaded.

He was much more organized than I in arranging for a party. One time, I was doing two things at once, as always. Pressed for time just before guests were due to arrive, I was heating a curling iron, and I decided to wash something in the basin at the same time. Well, you can imagine—I went right up in the air. On landing I rushed to Rosie, quivering all over.

"Rosie, I've been electrocuted!" I was still clutching the curling iron.

"You're still talking," he answered laconically.

It's hard to get hysterical with a husband like that.

He loved parties; that was the main reason I gave so many at Kinsale. He always wanted them to be outstanding successes and that, I think, is the secret of really fine entertaining. We had such whopping successes that we had to build the fanciest cabana that has ever adjoined a swimming pool—but more of that later.

While gardening and entertaining were *my* chief pleasures at Kinsale, Rosie loved to fish. This section of Florida is a great one for the angler, and periodically Isaak Walton's disciples would foregather and a big expedition would be afoot, or rather afloat. Little Pat was always indisposed—a headache, a sore throat or that tired feeling that can presage any old ailment.

As soon as the fishermen were out of sight, Pat was off to Palm Beach to have her hair done or engage in the feminine shopping that always infuriates a male companion. Or else I'd be out in the garden seeing if my plants and flowers, which were coming now from all over the world, were happy.

It's not that I can't fish. I've caught a lot of fish, from girlhood days in Newfoundland to trips off the Florida keys and in the Mediterranean. But for some reason I just didn't care to be cramped up in a fishing boat with maybe a little dead mackerel looking up at me as if it were saying, "Why did you do this to me?"

In addition to fishing, quail hunting was a great sport around Kinsale. Rosie loved this, too. I tried to join in briefly, but here I needed no excuses to stay at home when I discovered that the hunters might be after quail, but the snakes were after the hunters. I have a deadly fear of snakes. I was always appalled when one of them was caught and killed on Kinsale proper. I wasn't about to go looking for them.

As a matter of fact, I arranged, whenever possible, to have a doctor go along on one of Rosie's hunting expeditions. I would slip him an array of thermos bottles containing snake-bite serums. The men of course wore boots way up over their knees.

Curiously enough, we never had a boat at Kinsale. Rosie, as a Navy captain, was too used to big ships of the line, I suppose. Anyway many of our friends along the Florida coast had their own boats, and we were constantly being invited to go on cruises.

We never accepted except with the stipulation that we bring the lunch for an outing, and I can assure you that they were rather sumptuous repasts. Our regular pièce de résistance during the season was a ripe watermelon for dessert. We would cut a plug out of the melon and fill it with Piper Heidsick champagne and then plug it up again. Our maritime hosts always said, "We've never tasted such wonderful melon, Pat. Where did you get it? Did you grow it yourself?"

I'd always answer yes, and then tell them how I had especially cultivated it to bring out the full melon flavor!

When I write that we never had a boat, it isn't exactly true. We had a do-it-yourself boat long before amateur carpenters, builders and cabinet makers flourished everywhere. We had gone to a boat show, and out of curiosity Rosie picked up the designs for a skiff that we thought would look nice in the lagoon. We put it together in the garage. It took us three seasons to get the scow in shape. It certainly had experts involved in its construction—all sorts of Navy brass, friends of Rosie's, were pressed into service when they visited us. I remember helping to push it across the lawn and into the lagoon. It floated!

It was named Victor, for my Kinsale major domo. Victor is a Filipino who came with us to Florida from New York soon after we acquired Kinsale. He is a combination caretaker, cook, chauffeur, gardener, confidant and loyal friend. He runs Kinsale, and without him I don't think I would have kept the place after Rosie's death. The natives around Kinsale couldn't make Victor out when he first arrived, particularly the Negroes. Victor didn't bother to trace his antecedents but merely introduced himself, with a twinkle in his eye:

"I American Indian."

On the basis of this somewhat puzzling declaration Victor was accepted immediately and is extremely popular wherever he goes. He loves the movies and fishing and misses Chinese restaurants. He loves Kinsale. He misses the Captain very much. It gave me great solace to be able to talk to him about Rosie after I was able to face my loss to some extent.

It was at Kinsale that I learned to walk backwards. I've been doing a lot of it ever since. It came about partly from the way Rosie and I went about fixing up Kinsale at the beginning. We started outside the house and gradually moved in, working from the creek or the lagoon. I always walked backwards so that I would know what I was going to see coming out of our home. I even did it when I was planning my gardens up north. I even do it in my dreams. It was very important in designing the Westchester and Bahia Mar Candlelights, where I have so little land with which to work. I recommend it to any gardener. Walking backwards is hazardous at times, but it saves many mistakes in beautifying grounds, or even a back yard.

It was walking backwards that prompted our unusual entrance. I told Rosie: "We have to have something special for those who come to our beautiful Kinsale."

"I've got it," he said. "A red brick front step to contrast with the white crushed stone of the driveway."

"But we've got to repeat the white," I said firmly.

"All right, Pat," he agreed. "We'll have a white rug on the brick step."

And we've had a white rug there ever since.

Then, to complete the picture, he placed leprechauns at either side of the step. Guests got quite a welcome at Kinsale, and still do.

It was not merely walking backwards that made my landscaping at Kinsale somewhat celebrated in horticultural circles. I really experimented. First my fine twenty-seven-foot hill was made to seem much bigger by the use of steep inclines with beautiful rocks, and shrubbery that accented small elevations. Screened walks with steps leading down long inclines completed the illusion of a majestic promontory or headland.

As to my flowers, I guess I tried just about everything. Palm trees, including the great traveller's palm, the bark of which can be cut to get water in the desert, were an integral part of the planting and formed the background for the swimming pool before it was even built. It had the usual exotic semi-tropical blooms, including sunflowers from Switzerland and poppies from California as well as hollyhocks, primroses, forsythia and many other northern flowers that weren't supposed to grow in that part of Florida. I know that I had the local garden experts shaking their heads on more than one occasion.

In a place where everything grows twenty-four hours a day

ENTRANCE, KINSALE

GREENHOUSE, KINSALE

LIVING ROOM, KINSALE

DINING ROOM, KINSALE

I was willing to try acclimating blooms that were considered alien to Florida, such as roses, tulips, daffodils, lilies of the valley, and freesia, as well as oranges, gardenias and orchids. I had greenhouses of course, but I was frustrated on more than one occasion. Lots of alien species, I found, needed replanting each year in Florida, although they bloomed incessantly for their short span of life.

It was Otis who gave me a philosophical approach to the few failures I encountered at Kinsale. I had put in something which I was certain would thrive in the lush semi-tropical climate. It disappeared. With a knowing shake of his head my inherited gardener merely said, "It didn't want to grow, Mrs. Kiernan."

He was right. Always I have read garden books prodigiously. I even turned to an encyclopedia when I first took up one of my favorite pastimes—orchids. But, in the final analysis, it's a matter of looking at a plant or a flower and deciding whether or not it is happy. If it is, you're in business.

On the island, which was quite bare, I planted pines. When I found that the fisherfolk loved to pass our lagoon and even took refuge in it during storms, I had Rosie install concealed lighting so that it would give them added pleasure after dusk. Captain Kiernan was an extraordinarily adept amateur lighting expert. Top engineers from General Electric have come to Kinsale to see our illuminated gardens and lawns. Actually he started off with kerosene lanterns and wicks burning in pots of oil. They gave a lovely light, but electricity proved more practical.

The interior of Kinsale was furnished very, very slowly. We made do for several seasons with the furniture already there, gradually replacing pieces, until now one sofa is all that is left. In this way we were able to do each room properly from rugs to lights and finally achieve a harmonious whole. It was a lived-in house, too. I had learned to sew in the convent, but I found my seafaring husband was much better at it. He did all the darning and mending. He had bought some beautiful pajamas in Hong Kong, and in the course of time had sewn up a rent in the trousers. Then when they were about to fall apart, he sent them to the same tailor in Hong Kong, requesting him to copy them exactly. Back they came, together with a brand new pair complete with rent and darn.

The magnificent cabana behind the swimming pool was another of those wonderful gestures of Rosie's. He could complain about the cost of lawns and build his own boat, but at the same time would indulge my most expensive whims. He had originally planned a canvas bathhouse by the pool—a place to change into a swim suit and shower. We would have had just that except for one of my gala parties that really got out of hand. You know how parties are. Sometimes people are charming and well-behaved. But those same guests can become mighty wild on other occasions.

It was just such pandemonium that created real havoc in and around Kinsale. Rugs were ruined, furniture scarred, and shrubbery broken. Rosie surveyed the wreckage the next morning and said, "No canvas bathhouse, Pat. We're going to build a special place for parties."

That's how we got our beautiful cabana, with its great fireplace, marble wash basins, kitchenette, and built-in showers. Actually, it was just as elegant as Kinsale itself and could have been just as badly damaged by careless party guests. But we were lucky and had no more unruly galas.

Kinsale would not have been possible, of course, had my restaurant business not profited mightily. The Westchester Candlelight was more successful than all three of the original Candlelights combined. Rosie's Navy salary of $7,500 annually (a ridiculously inadequate sum for a captain in this country's service) would not have gone far at Kinsale.

But I like to think that Rosie and I would have found equal happiness during the golden years of our marriage in the small home I had imagined buying when we first were looking for Kinsale. I'm sure we would.

Chapter Ten

WESTCHESTER CANDLELIGHT

WHAT WE DID at Kinsale would not have been possible with my three-cornered merry-go-round in New York. Manhasset had been a huge success, grossing close to a million and a half dollars in its first year. The Candlelight on 60th Street continued to boom, and even Brooklyn Heights was showing a tidy profit. But to keep one's finger constantly on three such diverse establishments as these, catering to different tastes, supervising different kitchens and personnel with the sheer physical travel involved, was a time-and-a-half undertaking.

Rosie had rented a place on Long Island when the Manhasset Candlelight opened, but I soon found that I had no time to run a home of my own. We took an apartment at the Hotel Pierre as a sort of general headquarters for our enterprises. It was work, work, work and being so tired at the end of a day that I could hardly relax. Rosie knew I was getting near the breaking point.

"Pat," he said, "you've got a real country place now, but you haven't got time to enjoy it. Let's have one perfect Candlelight and give up this merry-go-round you're on."

It was a decision I don't think I could have made alone, but it appealed to me immediately. Only a short time earlier I had made a flying trip to Kinsale to see the century plants in bloom in late September, but it had thrown my schedule out of gear and I had to work twice as hard when I returned. Usually we would go South briefly in October to start the gardens, and then go back again in January for a few weeks. Kinsale was certainly too lovely and satisfying a home for this sort of nodding acquaintance.

So we disposed of our three glowing Candlelight restaurants and searched around for the perfect place for the perfect restaurant. Rosie was a native of Westchester and it was there that we started to prowl around, feeling that it was a centrally located, expanding county—just the right site. We had a very old, very beautiful house in mind and even planned the remodelling of it, but we ran into zoning problems. It was just as well that we did. The place wouldn't have been nearly big enough for a Westchester Candlelight, even with additions.

Finally we came across a bleak and forbidding hillside on Central Avenue, close to the New York Thruway, and I knew right away this was it. I guess, with this important step in my restaurant career, I wanted to start from scratch and cope with problems that were of my own making.

It required lots of mental walking backwards to plan this Candlelight. There wasn't a tree or a bush on the place when we took it over, but there was a hillside, a certain seclusion, and upwards of ten acres of land. At the time it seemed far too big, although almost before I knew it I was buying two more parcels of land. I had planned for a car lot in a park-like area full of trees and flowers. I badly underestimated the number of cars and buses that would converge on the Westchester Candlelight. There was no chance for a tree-shaded parking lot, and at one point Rosie was quite put out when I insisted on building a lake where we might have parked hundreds of autos.

We had fun right from the start in Westchester, creating a hillside of beauty and a place for gracious living where there had been absolutely nothing before. It took a lot of money—a million dollars and more before we were finished—but I have never gone back to this Candlelight without a deep feeling of pleasure and satisfaction, such as a creative artist must often feel. It presented so many difficulties and challenges. But solving them with Rosie at my side was a glorious adventure in business and living.

It is curious that when you start a big project which no one else thought of doing you are regarded with a combination of astonishment and resentment. The citizens of Yonkers (we thought we were in Bronxville and even had letterheads printed with Bronxville on them) were mighty puzzled when they saw their gloomy, rocky, vacant lot start to blossom forth. The local bankers thought we were crazy, investing such a large sum in such a risky business as a suburban dining place, and couldn't understand why we'd picked this spot for our restaurant. When the neighbors saw how profitable the Candlelight was they resented it and complained bitterly about the project, even though it increased real estate value and drew people to the town and shopping centers.

When we had the place about two-thirds completed, the zoning law was altered in some way so that all we could sell was food and liquor. I had started my greenhouses and had plans for a gift shop, but it took quite some time before I could open them to the public. The day before we opened there was a threat of making the whole district purely residential, but I marched in with all my medals and trophies, not to mention my best feminine wiles, and put a stop to that. Here was the biggest restaurant in the East, serving more than 5,000 people daily and bringing customers to the town, increasing real estate values 400 per cent, and beautifying a formerly barren and forbidding district, and still narrow-minded people tried to stop it.

No matter. It was a fabulous success from the start. To a gal who had started in counting thin dimes in a pint-sized Brooklyn restaurant, this Westchester Candlelight seemed so big, so tremendous. Not only did it fill to capacity but we had to start expanding right away, and I've been doing it ever since. My plan was to begin on one floor with dining rooms part way up our rocky hill, a lake in front and gardens on all sides. Since I had wanted an old place originally, I had the idea of building balconies around the front to make the building look more lived in, but these had to be closed in right away to make more dining space, while a second floor was added.

The planting gave me as much joy as anything in Westchester. The first winter I put $169,000 into landscaping. Rosie asked me one day:

"You're such a strange girl, Pat, I'm wondering what to give you for a present. Do you want a new fur coat or a greenhouse?"

Without a second's hesitation, I answered, "A greenhouse, Captain!"

As a matter of record I got both the greenhouse and the fur coat. It was a very large and quite famous nursery which had gone to pot to the extent of losing $32,000 the year before I took it over. Again as a matter of record, it made $30,000 the first year I operated it. This astounded Rosie.

"What are you doing with orchids and all that sort of stuff, Pat?" he said. "Your business is selling mashed potatoes."

Maybe I like orchids better than mashed potatoes. I still remember that evening in Brooklyn when I debated long with myself whether to buy a little bunch of flowers or a square meal. For another thing, I never wanted to make anything out of my venture into horticulture. I'm tremendously pleased today to take people, particularly groups of school children, through the 60,000 tulips that bloom in the spring, the 10,000 chrysanthemums that cover the hillside in the fall or the greenhouses full of exotic orchids and other plants, even when they don't spend a penny in the place.

We opened the Westchester Candlelight on September 24th, 1954. Any good restaurant proprietor will tell you that time of year is the worst possible time to launch a suburban dining spot. We hadn't advertised. We didn't have a sign and we had very few lights, but people came right in and we were jammed. I thought we had the biggest dining room and kitchen ever, but we have had to enlarge them three times since we opened, and now I'm putting on a receiving room addition to the kitchen just to handle incoming food.

One of Rosie's big gestures for my comfort in having "a place for everything and everything in its place" was to have been "Pat's private office, dressing room and shower." I had it for a few months; then the boiler room started moving in on my dressing room and the public address system, by which diners are told when and where they can be seated according to their arrival, started moving in on my office. I still have a little corner, to be sure, done in pale yellow silk, but it is scarcely a spot for relaxation. The thing I remember most vividly, though, about the hectic expansion during the phenomenal early success in Westchester, was the safe.

It was a long time ago that I had hidden my receipts in a coffee pot along with a varied assortment of pans in Brooklyn Heights. A spanking big safe was installed in my office and I wondered how we could ever use all that space for currency. Well, business became so big that we gradually had three big safes, one piled on the other. When we first planned Westchester I had certain regrets about giving up three profitable restaurants and settling for one. But the new Candlelight is over twice the size of my Manhasset place and bigger by far than all three original Candlelights put together.

We always had great fun planning and operating the Westchester Candlelight, and I think our pleasure communicated itself. The first Christmas we had a very mild crowd of celebrants, singing carols and behaving very decorously. This was before I installed the Snow Queen, and the crèche with live sheep, and frosted the trees and bushes on the hillside. Anyway, the neighbors, who were determined to object to an upstart restaurateur, and a woman at that, moving in on them, started telephoning in complaints. I visited all of them, assured them I hadn't meant to disturb them, and kept the singing at a minimum. Now these people are my good friends and point with pride to the Candlelight.

What is even more remarkable is the fact that prospective diners, who have to take their turn for seats in the Gold Room, Crystal Room or Garden Room according to the time of their arrival, will wait for an hour or more and have fun waiting. They can visit the cocktail lounge, where we serve shrimps and canapes with the drinks, the greenhouse and the gift shop, or wander through the paths on the hillside, banked spectacularly during the tulip and chrysanthemum season with quince, plum, dogwood, Japanese cherry and dozens of other shrubs, trees and plants. They can even stock up for the next day's breakfast with the crisp and crunchy little loaves of bread which are served on a bread board with a knife at every table, and with jellies and jams. On a busy day it is not unusual to have more than a thousand customers waiting for seating at one time. In the parking lots there are apt to be twenty or thirty buses from all over, bringing clubs or other groups to ceremonial dinners, as well as hundreds of private cars. A Mercedes-Benz lounge car whisks customers right up to the entrance.

Of course we had our problems. During the hurricane floods of '56 our whole hill was almost washed away, and I'll never forget itemizing the floating debris in our lake as though it wouldn't all be cleaned up and everything put to rights as soon as the torrential storm subsided. That was still my failing—a fear of the unknown. It was Rosie who saved me from many anxious hours during those first years in Westchester. When an expensive piece of machinery broke down it was always, "Send for the Captain."

Being an engineer, he was able to supervise and understand any repair job that had to be made. I would have thrown up my hands and allowed the experts to take me for any amount of work that they had cared to do on a job. In this respect the Westchester Candlelight was a vast relief for me and a real chance to take it at a slightly more relaxed pace. One time when 60th Street was at its busiest hour, the heating system had broken down in Brooklyn. I can still remember the curious stares that greeted me as I made my way by subway carrying two electric heaters to keep customers from freezing on Brooklyn Heights. No longer was my business a matter of "making do."

We had a fire—a small roof fire, which occurred at an awkward time. It was during the Christmas season and we had more than 1,250 customers, not counting several hundred employees and hundreds of diners waiting to have their names called over the p.a. system. I had arranged a great burst of lights on the roof to illuminate the wonderful Christmas decorations that we had all around the Candlelight. When I heard the running of feet on the roof I knew that the worst had happened. At a time like this I knock on wood and prepare to meet the Fire Department. Fortunately, Rosie turned the right switches and made for the roof with some blankets and fire extinguishers. As he was making his way upstairs, my sister Sheila rushed up to him.

"Oh, Captain," she said, "I've got to have one of those blankets. One of the sheep in the crèche has just had a lamb."

"Later, sister, later," were his calm words. He had the fire under control in a matter of minutes. And no one in all the hundreds of customers in the Candlelight had an inkling that there had been a fire during their period of dining and wining.

The gift shop was Rosie's idea. He always referred to it as "the jewel in Patsy's crown." He wanted a little crystal palace for me and it is just that. It was quite an expensive little palace, for the surveyor had made a mistake about our line and we had done a lot of building before I discovered the mistake and moved the gift shop back. The fellow on whose land we were poaching knew it all the time, but figured that his little strip of land would be worth a whopping sum when the gift shop was completed. As it was it cost us some $30,000 to move it back.

In any account of the Westchester Candlelight there must be mention of the wonderful help we always had. We always employed a lot of youngsters going to school, or young married couples, and of course they needed the money and would work very hard to get ahead. I always gave a bonus of $50 or $75 to the room that had the biggest turnover, and working so much myself in the place from the start, I was able to promote the personnel properly. But that doesn't explain waitresses, hostesses and even kitchen help arriving early on especially busy days and working late at night for no extra money. Everybody pulled together even though we had an assorted crew always—Filipinos, local Westchester kids, an Arab in the kitchen. I've tried to help youngsters by sending them for more schooling. Usually they came back to the Candlelight. When Rosie died, their affection and loyalty moved me deeply.

Without them I could not have carried on after the first terrible shock. The Westchester Candlelight was too big for two hands, even if those hands belonged to a rather energetic woman. It lived up to all the expectations we had had for it when we disposed of my other Candlelights. Principally it gave us a few years at the end in which we could enjoy ourselves together without the constant worry and work we were obliged to put into running three places.

We went to Florida a lot before Captain Kiernan's death. Usually we reserved two drawing rooms—one for us and one for the flowers. When the porters saw me coming, either in New York or Florida, they'd say, "Here she comes again, with all those plants!"

For I'd take things from the greenhouses in Westchester and try them out at Kinsale. And then I'd bring back all sorts of tropical flowers to the Candlelight, stacking them to the very ceiling of the railway car bedroom. I used some for exhibits, including the large one I had at the New York Coliseum, but principally we wanted to share the beauty of tropical foliage with northerners at the Westchester Candlelight who'd never imagined such exotic flowers. It didn't start as an educational program, but it turned out to be one—for the people who came to the Candlelight primarily to see the surroundings, for ordinary customers, and for me. Today I can look at almost any plant and know if it is going to do well.

The hillside was very important to me in creating the Westchester Candlelight just as the slight elevation at Kinsale gave a special quality to the landscaping. The rocky hill on Central Avenue was as important to me as the fact that this was the largest tract of land available close to a network of thoroughfares.

I've always thought that obsession to possess a flowering hillside was a direct reaction to my girlhood in a Newfoundland fishing village. There we had to hunt for soil to put in Nana's garden, taking long boat trips at times to get the precious loam. We were surrounded by flat beaches with stones that we heated and used as bed warmers. The Westchester Candlelight was the fulfillment of a childhood dream to climb a flowering hillside and fairly swim in beautiful blooms.

Chapter Eleven

THE LIGHTS GO OUT

When rosie died the world collapsed—not just my lovely private world; everything that lived or moved within my consciousness faded away. At least people were so distant and so detached that they were meaningless.

The doctors called it "a state of shock," and my sainted mother and beloved sister Sheila seemed to be constantly engaged in whispering consultations to no avail.

It seems that I was able to make decisions in preparation for the final rites, but, fortunately, I remember very little about the ghastly days before the Captain's funeral.

Unwittingly, I began to let a barrier grow around me. In fact, I was helping to build it stronger and stronger to make a safe place for my retreat. My one instinct was to keep people at a distance, to close out their "comfort," which seemed to be the most outrageous intrusion of my privacy.

Flashes of memory come back to torture me: the deep gloom of St. Patrick's Cathedral on that interminable day; the sharp ringing sound of the naval salute at Arlington Cemetery—final tribute and high honor to Captain James Kiernan of the U.S. Navy.

Standing stiffly at attention under the open sky, I felt an overwhelming numb despair. I knew that I was alone.

Perhaps grief is selfish; if so, I made the most of it from that moment on.

At one point, someone, in good faith, pressed my hand and murmured something about "courage." What stupidity. Courage was for men at war, for women with small children to be cared for; courage was for people who must face life against great odds; sometimes it was necessary for survival. It was a vacant word for me. What I really longed for was some kind of catastrophe, violent and swift, something that would overtake me and do away with this unfamiliar pain.

What I really wanted was oblivion.

But many women who have been in my position—suddenly widowed—know that oblivion is not to be had for the asking. They know that the grief and despair, no matter how unbearable at first, give way to a bitter acceptance of half-living and a sort of numb renewal of daily routine.

This happened to me gradually as I took up the old tasks of keeping the Westchester Candlelight gay and hospitable and tending to a few of my many other interests. Most of my activity was purely reflex action, and could be stopped dead by the sudden realization of my great loss.

In large measure this was because Captain Kiernan—Rosie—was so utterly different from me, although we lived and worked so closely together for nearly a decade. It was not part of me that was missing, as I unwillingly faced each new day through that black, desolate period. It was a wonderful extension of me that was gone, an ability to look at the world, people, personal problems, through different eyes, and achieve the great and enduring magic of living with another person and sharing his innermost thoughts and feelings.

I was a born gambler, ready to shoot the works on a business venture or a purely personal decision. Rosie was solidly conservative, trained with the great and rigid discipline of the Navy, one to consider every aspect of a situation before making a decision. I was all out for gaiety and frivolity once I knew that I wasn't going to be hungry tomorrow, come what might. He was serious and thoughtful, even in his relaxed moods, as befitted an architect, engineer, and commander of men. I didn't change much during our marriage—neither did he. But I think we both benefited extraordinarily from the fact that we came together from somewhat different poles and were able to extend one another's experience.

For many, many months remembrance of our lives together made my grief more profound and seemingly insupportable. I turned to my work. This was one time when I was very grateful that I had the habit of keeping time filled. This is a great advantage that those of us who have had to work and sweat for a living have at a time of desperate loss and desolation. My routine was so fixed by this time that it was almost second nature to busy myself with the Candlelight and the plans that Rosie and I had put in progress.

But I was moving about like an automaton, going to Westchester to supervise my restaurant, returning to Kinsale when I became tired and ill from working too hard with no relaxation, without that wonderful opportunity I had of turning to someone when problems arose, when tension built up to a point where I just couldn't face my problems.

There were a few rare friends who helped me through the terribly blank despondency of sudden widowhood. I shall never forget their kindness and understanding. One of them, who is known to the general public only as a too-rich and idle woman with a stable of horses as her chief preoccupation, was uncommonly thoughtful. She never let a day go by without telephoning me from the race track, her home, or wherever she might be. She never mentioned Rosie. She never mentioned my loss. Just a cheery greeting and some idle chit-chat about her horses, the weather or the latest headlines or gossip columns. It may sound odd to those who have not been in the position of not really wanting to live, but these seemingly trivial telephone calls did much to pull me out of my grief.

And then, very slowly, came the time when remembrance of Rosie became a positive, rewarding thing. I recalled a day, just an ordinary day, we had spent together. It was in the late '40s, after he had finished a job of research for the government—a job, incidentally, for which he got a large sum, which he promptly sent back to the Navy Department. He didn't go off to work, like most husbands. But we could be so busy together that we never had time to talk to each other!

If we were at the Candlelight, he would be in the office, devising a new p.a. system or figuring out how we could get more parking space. I would be in the kitchen, planning menus, supervising the hundreds of young men and women we now had working at the place. We'd meet briefly to go over the budget, or plan expenditures for new machinery or additions. We would both work hard and, curiously enough, be very happy just knowing that the other was near. Even at home for many years we'd spend lots of time in different rooms.

He didn't like the theater or the movies, so he'd sit and listen to the news reports on the radio and read, while I'd watch the shows on television. Then when General MacArthur made his famous speech about old generals just fading away, I found I could get him to look at news on TV, particularly if some famous personage was appearing, whether he knew him or not, whether he liked him or not. And then after the news or the Army-Navy football game, which was another TV lure for him, we might just sit quietly together and do nothing. Isn't that the way with many married couples?

At Kinsale we were always busy together, whether we were fixing the place, giving parties or gardening. I tended to the rare and beautiful plants while Rosie, always the engineer, would be installing new hidden lights to pick up lovely corners of Kinsale after dark.

I remember driving into Stuart and finding him chatting with a couple of neighbors on the street corner. Never have I seen such a disreputable trio, dressed in old khakis, frayed shirts and sloppy hats. I stopped the car and hailed them. Both Rosie's friends were big tycoons and millionaires several times over.

"To look at you three," I said, "one would think you didn't have two nickels to rub together between the three of you."

These memories crowded in on me as I stopped being plain numb, and I found them warming and almost gay as I went about the Candlelight or Kinsale. And then came memories of our travels together. Rosie had been all over the world and was a wonderful companion. He would always avoid the tourist traps, taking me down side streets and to little out-of-the-way shops where I'd find exciting things to buy. He'd rather bargain than buy things, and even in New York he'd walk through celebrated jewelry stores looking at everything but rarely making a purchase. He was so handsome and affluent looking that I'm sure the salesmen always thought they'd make a sale on one of his tours of inspection.

He would buy rare stones for me—where, I'll never know—and then have them made up in stunning rings, brooches or what have you. I have a jewel box full of these unique and thoughtful gifts. When we were in Rome one time I was having my hair done. He wouldn't set foot in a beauty salon usually, but this time he came charging in (while I was still under the dryer) with a lovely emerald in one hand, a rare orchid in the other.

His brother came to me one time and asked, "Isn't Rosie spending an awful lot of money on presents, Pat?"

Rosie overheard him. He wasn't really angry, but he was very firm as he put a hand on John's shoulder and said, "All I can do is to give Pat everything I have. You see, this is the way I want it. When that's gone there isn't any more, but I'll do anything I can to make her happy while it's there."

One wonderful thing I remembered about travelling with Rosie was the fact that he took complete charge. Tickets, passports, reservations, keys, money, letters of credit were his responsibility; I never gave them a thought. This was embarrassing on one occasion.

We had gone down to Washington from New York for the Inaugural Ball in 1957 and I had taken a van-load of luggage, all my finery and jewelry, much more than I needed. We were in the station the next day and, while the porter was loading the drawing room, Rosie went off to check on the tickets. It was foggy on the platform. I got panicky just before the train was due to pull out and had the porter take all the baggage off. There was still no Rosie. I went to the stationmaster's office. Believe it or not, I didn't have enough money to telephone anyone.

I was dressed fit to kill, since we had come from a big cocktail party where we were in the receiving line. I was wearing a lovely lamé dress, emeralds, mink coat—and not a nickel! The stationmaster was pretty baffled, but he got on the phone and found out that Rosie had boarded our train and was waiting for me at Arlington.

"I'll have to have some money," I said, "to get a ticket."

He became very suspicious, and was even more so when I offered to make out a blank check. He said he might lend me a couple of dollars. Indignantly, rattled as I was, I answered: "I'm not the sort of person you lend a couple of dollars to!"

He finally let me have five dollars and I boarded the next train to Arlington. I barely had enough money to tip the porter. Of course, I thought Rosie was going to scalp me. It was all my fault. But he only laughed at me and sent the five dollars to the stationmaster. It was the only time we were ever separated.

After a time the memories of small incidents meant as much to me as the larger aspects of our married life.

Then there was the championship horse Rosie bought for me in Ireland and then kept himself. He was named Treaty Stone, and won ribbons every time he was shown. I understood perfectly why Rosie kept him. He was no rider, having had a disastrous experience the only time he was on a horse while he was attached to the British Navy in the early years of the war. When he found out that Treaty Stone was for showing, not riding, he decided that this was for him, and gave me another thoroughbred instead.

And I remember the map of the world that I had painted on the wall of our apartment on East 60th Street. On it I had decorated each and every place that Rosie had been in his travels with the Navy or in the course of his work as an architect and engineer. One day I was showing the map to a friend, and was pointing out the exotic spots in the Orient when Rosie walked up.

"Pat, that map's wrong," he said. He was meticulously honest.

"What's wrong?"

"You see that island off the China coast? I never was actually there, although I was awfully close. And this town in Cambodia, I wasn't there."

Jack Lynas had to fix up the wall map, you can be sure. I wish he had done it on muslin, so I could still have it.

As memories flooded back, I realized that this was as it should be, that this was, in a sense, life after death for one to whom I had been very close. I was able to talk to Nana about Rosie. They had a wonderfully "friendly enemy" relationship, always taking each other to task in humorous fashion and blaming each other for everything, including the state of the world, but held together by a fierce devotion. I found Nana could talk about Rosie as though he were just away on a trip, and this gave me great comfort.

Finally, I resolved to carry through all the plans we had made together. My learning to fly my own plane was not on the schedule, but everything else that has been done in the last few years had been envisioned by both of us. In fact, I do not think I would have had the courage or strength to tackle some of these projects without remembering how enthusiastic he had been in the early planning stages.

Whatever I do in the future will be governed in part by my desire to keep his memory alive. One can tote up material success in terms of dollars and physical rewards. They can add up to an impressive monument to hard work and ingenuity. But it is the personal factors of living that make up the measure of one's true success.

Chapter Twelve

NEW ADVENTURES

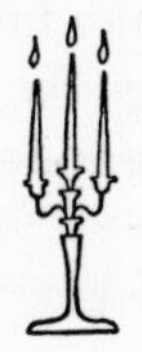

EVEN THE RELIVING of golden memories is small solace for widowhood. The sudden loss of one so close to me was far more than an emotional shock. Even when I was able to talk to people about Rosie and engage again in the daily routines which had made our lives so happy, at the Candlelight or at Kinsale, I found myself physically depleted. So it was that I put off for a time the partly formulated plans we had made for the future. Some people might call this running away from grief. I prefer to think of it as shaking off an obsession and gathering strength for the undertakings Rosie and I had planned together.

There was an Irish interlude which was as happy an excursion as any could have been at the time. I rented a lovely old country place, Castle MacGarrett in Claremorris, and for the first time was able to mingle with people as a hostess again and attend parties. Being quite a large castle, it was able to accommodate lots of my friends. I had twenty-two house guests at one time during the Galway Race Week. The American Ambassador was entertained and I had the Irish Pipers down from

Dublin. Memories of Rosie crowded around me even here in Ireland, for his great horse, Treaty Stone, was selected to try out at Harewood, England, for the Olympics, and I loaned him to the Irish Army to compete in international horse shows.

The high point of this trip, though, was the great delight that it gave Nana. I had not thought she would want to make the journey, but it required very little persuasion. She had been so close to me and so understanding that I immediately booked passage on the Queen Elizabeth for Nana and my secretary of 28 years, Elsie Tineo.

"You're flying, aren't you, Pat?" she asked, and I told her I'd chartered a plane for my guests.

"If you're flying, I'll fly," said Nana. "I want to jet once before I die."

And jet she did. The comparative lack of privacy on the plane was the only thing that bothered her, and she remained dressed to the teeth crossing the Atlantic. Once when the pilot came back to see if we were comfortable, she made me button my jacket. I'm surprised she didn't make me put a hat on.

In Ireland, she was in her element. When the pipers arrived from Dublin and started playing reels, she didn't miss a jig. After the Claremorris interlude I sent her to London and the continent, getting a car and chauffeur to make it easier for her to visit a few cities. A few cities! She did the grand tour as it has rarely been done.

Earlier that year I had my minor triumph at the Coliseum International Flower Show, with the famous $25,000 carousel of 5,000 orchids, another escape from the persistent memories of Rosie. And while I was in Ireland I was able to read in the United States Naval Academy Alumni Association magazine, *Shipmate*: "The Class of '19's Memorial Stadium Gate, one of the two flanking the east stands, was provided through the generosity of Mrs. James E. Kiernan." Under the Class Seal on its handsome bronze plaque is the inscription:

IN MEMORY OF CAPTAIN JAMES EUGENE KIERNAN UNITED STATES NAVY AND IN HONOR OF THE CLASS OF 1919, UNITED STATES NAVAL ACADEMY.

When I returned from Ireland in late summer, I was ready to take up again where Rosie and I as a team had left off, always having our joint plans in mind, always having him present in spirit and in project wisdom to guide me in decisions and give me strength in new undertakings.

At the Westchester Candlelight I found his memory very much alive. The Arab kitchen worker prayed regularly for the Captain, with his face turned towards Mecca, and all my wonderful youngsters were not only solicitous of me but would occasionally break out with: "Now what would the Captain have done now?"

The main problem was that of space and keeping crowds of customers (sometimes over 1,000) happy while waiting for tables. I expanded both the dining rooms and the parking sites —this for the third time since the Candlelight opened. The lovely Jewel Box gift shop is a favorite gathering place of guests waiting to hear their names called for a table, and so is the greenhouse where they can buy orchids, plants and bouquets for a song. When you realize that there are sometimes fifty or more buses from distant towns parked at one time, you can see that customers are really grateful to be able to get more than food.

That old "atmosphere," which I once thought meant the weather, has become more and more an outstanding feature of the restaurant. Holidays are traditional at the Candlelight. I have always made much of them from the early days in Brooklyn, perhaps because of my bitter disappointment when the Russian "princess" at Mr. & Mrs. Foster's refused to let me look at the St. Patrick's Day parade. But never did I have such a setting for celebrating as in Westchester.

I really don't know how many thousands of people come back year after year to see the Candlelight decked out for Thanksgiving, Christmas, St. Valentine's Day, or Easter. If you mingle with the crowds you will hear comparisons with former holiday decorations as well as exclamations of delight at a first viewing. I am so happy that many elderly people, particularly those living near by with not enough to splurge on a dinner, merely walk around or sit, drinking in the beauties of the place. I like to sit with them and see to it that they have some simple refreshments to enjoy while admiring the scene.

At Thanksgiving, the 400 employees are dressed up as Pilgrims and Indians and there are pumpkins, chrysanthemums, bittersweet, and clusters of brightly-colored Indian corn, mixed with autumn flowers. A male greeter is dressed as a Pilgrim Father, and pretty girls in white-hooded coats are on hand to direct traffic. Once I heard a man in a hurry, who was bucking the incoming guests, blurt out: "You even have to wait to get *out* of here!"

In the kitchen dozens of chefs and helpers serve an endless line of waitresses as more than hundreds of 25-pound turkeys are sliced, in addition to all the other entrees dished up. A thousand cars are in the vast expanses of the parking lots, with buses clustered in one corner. On some holidays I suddenly stop with a slight shiver as I figure up that, counting the help, there are 2,500 persons on the premises at one time.

Christmas is very special at the Candlelight. And no one has described it more beautifully, I think, than the celebrated food editor of the *New York Herald Tribune,* Clementine Paddleford, to whom, incidentally, I have dedicated a rare new variety of orchid which bears her name. Herewith is her account of a visit a year or so ago:

Driving up Central Park Avenue into Yonkers we come suddenly to a Christmas fairyland. Here are strings of lights. Spires of light blazing with color against a night drop curtain of deep purple.

Eleven trees we counted shouting Merry Christmas, each adorned with red and blue balls lighted within to twinkle like stars; so large and brilliant they made a weight of glory in the sky. This is the setting for Patricia Murphy's Candlelight Restaurant, a place brimming with people who have come to look and have brought the children along. This is the sixth year Patricia has created a wonderland for the holiday season. Families drive for miles to lift wondering eyes and find the spirit of Christmas.

Groups come by chartered busloads to admire and then enjoy a holiday dinner. Next Saturday, 1,827 people are scheduled for arrival from Hartford, Conn., from Perth Amboy, from Staten Island, from New Brunswick, N.J., from Schenectady, N.Y.

Enter the restaurant and go down a white corridor, its ceiling dripping frosted pine boughs, downy as feathers. On either side white snowflakes, no two alike. Enter the wide foyer which opens to the bar, separated only by a bank of poinsettias. Meet the Fairy Queen, young and beautiful, in white evening gown, the bouffant skirt scattered with stars. She is seated in a red velvet sleigh drawn by white doves attached to white satin ribbon reins. Wings are spread ready for flight into blue heaven.

Toss a coin into the silver fountain, a small donation for the Heart Foundation, and make a Christmas wish.

We stop to admire the Christmas tree, picked with care from the outdoor gardens to come inside for the grand occasion of Christmas. It stands in a deep wooden box of earth, its weight more than two tons. Ten men labored to bring the tree from garden to foyer. Two girls worked two days to hang more than 2,000 tree trims from every part of the world.

Between the reception room and the crystal dining room is a six foot tree, constructed of every seasonable fruit; apples, grapes, pears, pomegranates, tangerines, kumquats—and at the top a plumed pineapple, symbol of hospitality.

In the bar swags of fruit and flowers with candles are arranged against the mirrors. The bottles are gone from the back-bar glass shelves, replaced by hundreds of vesper candles glowing in variegated colors. From the ceiling comes the sparkle of stars to flame upon the heads of merry-makers.

Down an arcade bordered with pink begonias growing in snow we come to the Crystal Palace. This is a glass-walled room and glass-domed, filled with rare gifts from far places: Irish hand-woven scarves, Venetian glass figures.

Patricia Murphy, the creator of this Christmas paradise, led us from one glowing room into another. Each candle was lighted with a view into the decorated grounds. There thousands of lights were shining in the winter night, like glowworms, each winking a spark of gold. We could scarcely stop sight-seeing to take time for dinner. This was served in the Crystal Room where three tremendous chandeliers are joined by swags looking like shirred sleeves of pink silk and decorated with pink metal roses from Florence, Italy. Tables wear pink damask. Pink poinsettias everywhere. Two sides of the room are windowed, you look into the fairyland beyond pink holly leaves for wall covering. Walls throughout the restaurant are done with imitation holly in silver, pink and green. The leaves are threaded on strings and draped from ceiling to floor, hung overlapping to give the effect of a solid wall covering.

Dinner came and it was the same good food as always, but so elegantly served by pretty young women wearing sparkling tiaras and gold cloth aprons. The hostesses this Christmas are in dark green taffeta, their dresses designed by Suzy Perette.

The menu hasn't changed but somehow it tasted better than ever, by being seasoned with holiday cheer. For one the children wouldn't wait for dessert. They preferred to be outdoors to see the crèche with its live baby lambs. The visit to the carousel was saved for the last. "Jingle bells, jingle bells" came clear and merry. The reindeer drawing Santa's sleigh leaped in the air as lambs in the springtime. Curving silvered antlers, silver hoofs, long noble faces, eyes like laughing stars. And Santa Claus was laughing. Such joy is infectious and the children laughed too. The air was ringing with laughter. Beyond was the pool, a dark patch of indigo, reflecting a million stars of light.

On Valentine's Day, the Snow Queen of Christmas becomes a Queen of Hearts. This is a favorite holiday for youngsters, who marvel at the live ducks in the lake, just as they delighted at the real sheep in the Christmas crèche. I'm not sure what one would call the spring holiday. It's really a continuation of the Easter festivities when a pretty hostess presides over the gardens, really resplendent with the great masses of tulips which give way in June to bank upon bank of roses. Personal occasions are not neglected at the Candlelight. Anyone considering a birthday celebration has only to notify the reservations desk and, at the appropriate time, waitresses and popover girls sing "Happy Birthday to You" with a real feeling of conviviality about the proceedings.

There is no question that satisfied customers send other customers to Westchester, and even convince clubs and organizations to journey some distances for special luncheons and dinners. Since Rosie and I opened the Candlelight with no fanfare at all, and not even proper lighting, I have never bothered with advertising in a big way, being content to let patrons write postcards to friends.

But I am always very pleased when guests come back time after time to renew their pleasure in the place. I have a letter from one lady which I cherish. It reads in part:

"When you took over the first Candlelight Restaurant on Henry Street, I was your first customer (or very nearly the first). We lived at the St. George. It was a luncheon for some old aunts and my mother-in-law. Two years later you filled my apartment on Columbia Heights with exquisite flowers when our baby boy was born. That was twenty-eight years ago. I have never had so many lovely flowers at one time.

"My husband's family has a dinner every month. We take turns. I had my spring dinner and my fall dinner at your Westchester Candlelight. We come from widely separated spots. I am enthralled with the beauty of your gardens and the flowers."

The flowers bloom for most of the year outdoors and the seven greenhouses allow me to beat the cold winter months with masses of blossoms throughout the restaurant. At Kinsale it is twelve months of spectacular blooming. Since I have been able to spend much more time in Florida, as Rosie always wished, the gardens have become a spectacular year-round flower show. I have continued the planting around the cabana and across the illuminated "hillside" as he and I planned, and have added foliage to what a friend of mine calls "Blooming Island" beyond the lagoon. My devoted Victor, very much at home in the semi-tropical climate, grows papaya and other indigenous Filipino plants for his own amusement.

And Nana, who resides in state in a lovely canal-side bungalow in Fort Lauderdale, has a charming little garden which she runs independently of me and somewhat unconventionally. Like her own immaculate grooming (she has never been in a beauty parlor in her life) she has her own ideas about horticulture. Scorning newfangled fertilizers, she wanders down to the fishing wharves and buys five pounds of shark, which she buries deep to nurture a banana tree. When the shark isn't to be had she will substitute several pounds of calves' liver. And let me tell you, her garden really blooms.

She is a wonderful hostess, too, but never allows her guests, including me, to invade her little kitchen. It is there she keeps "the Lord's bottle," brought from the castle in Ireland, or so she says, to be poured on special occasions. Never a day goes by that I don't talk to her on the phone, although she is constantly indignant at the extravagance of my calling her from New York.

As I have mentioned, Kinsale has grown more lovely as the planting has come into maturity. Every time I look at the cabana or lunch beside the pool I am reminded of Rosie, who, with some sixth sense, put in a row of stately palms as a background before the cabana was even built. He would love the total effect today, and he is always in my thoughts as I am more and more able to enjoy the pervading beauty of the place with increased leisure and quiet meditation. One part of Kinsale remains exactly as it was before he died—his room. With its gracious Oriental pieces and his honors and trophies, it is a tangible setting for his ever-present spirit.

With far more time to spend at Kinsale and the challenge of opening a new restaurant, Bahia Mar, in Fort Lauderdale, I do much flying. It is a strange avocation for a widow with a host of other activities to occupy her attention, but it has given me a great lift out of my grief and a wonderful awareness of a new dimension to the world we live in. When I am flying down the Florida coast in "Miss Tango," watching the endless variety of cloud and sun patterns on the land and the ocean, when I am winging to Westchester or across to Nassau, I find a peace and serenity that I do not believe I could have achieved in any other manner. Rosie and I never discussed it, but I am certain that he would have approved.

Not entirely by design or forethought, the Westchester Candlelight and my relatively new marina restaurant, Bahia Mar, have quite different seasons. By having transportation always at hand with the speedy "Miss Tango," personnel and even food and flowers can be shifted north or south at peak periods. It still gives me a thrill to have Florida hibiscus, camellias, and orchids on view in Westchester or at Sky High in a matter of hours, or have tulips, forsythia, and primroses blooming in Florida at the same time they are in season in New York, gaily decorating my penthouse.

Sky High is a venture which Rosie and I kept putting off, probably because we were always working so hard and had Kinsale for brief periods of relaxation. It is about as close to having a country house in the heart of the city as one could imagine. Enormous terraces surround this penthouse on upper Fifth Avenue, which overlooks Central Park with a glimpse of the Hudson, the East River, mid-Manhattan and the Bronx. While opening up the interior (one wall with twin windows in the dining room was boxed in by a huge cupboard) and decorating and furnishing it graciously, I eagerly attacked the terraces, planting backgrounds of evergreens and flowering fruit trees and then putting in great masses of flowers to bloom in rotation. Chrysanthemums blossom way into the fall, and such hardy plants as geraniums and some varieties of roses and tulips take up the salute to color at the end of winter.

Indoors there are always arrangements of cut flowers and clusters of my favorite orchids, of which I now have so many species that it would be difficult to enumerate all of them. With a great dining room and an enormous living room, Sky High is ideal for entertaining. I only regret that Rosie and I had to settle for hotel living when we were New Yorkers. He would have delighted in the penthouse with its flowering frame, which he would have named the Hanging Garden of Babylon. Sky High is very practical too. I have a den which is really an office, and it is only a short distance to the Westchester Candlelight, where I spend most of the daylight and evening hours when I am in the North.

It is at Sky High that I participate in the City Garden Club annual spring showing of gardens and penthouse terraces. This is a project which provides scholarships and aids for public school teachers so that they may better stimulate natural science appreciation. My exhibit is called "Flowers in the Sky." Tropicals are grouped around a naturalistic fountain. Oleander and hibiscus lead to an area of ivy accented by primroses, violets and clematis. An old-fashioned garden of pansies, candytuft and miniature apple trees faces east, and to the south is an herb garden, planned for practicability as well as beauty, and including strawberries!

So much for Sky High. It is a wonderful city retreat for one who has always been torn between the charm of country and challenge of urban working and living.

Even though it is relatively new, I am deeply attached to my latest restaurant, the Bahia Mar, on the side of the Fort Lauderdale yacht basin. It took quite a bit of doing at the

TERRACE, SKY HIGH

DINING ROOM, SKY HIGH

DRAWING ROOM, SKY HIGH

start. I completely rebuilt and redesigned a drabby broken-down restaurant, installing three spacious dining rooms, and a long cool cocktail lounge and bar, where succulent shrimps and other hors d'oeuvres accompany drinks, as they do at the Westchester Candlelight. From the entrance through the foyer there is a spotlighted fountain. The side walls are banked with orchids except at Christmastime. The interior decorating has followed nature, the upholstery and drapes picking up and accenting the colors of rare and exotic semi-tropical flowers.

Around the Bahia Mar I have had to "make do" again with a minimum of space but I believe I have created quite an illusion of depth and distance, bringing the Marina in as background and centering attention in the small garden or a brook and pond. At any rate my customers are delighted with the "atmosphere" of Bahia Mar, and already I have a host of repeaters. As with all my Candlelights, this one burned brightly from the very outset with a minimum of promotion. The gift shop and the cocktail lounge are favorites of guests, and there are always crowds of patient and happy customers waiting their turns at tables. Without any exaggeration I think I can say that business at the Bahia Mar compares favorably with and even excels any other restaurant in Florida.

This is what happened to me, a teen-ager from a Newfoundland fishing village. Through the years, I have attempted to bring gracious living to many guests; now, through these pages, I hope to share with you my hard-earned knowledge of nature, beauty and experience.

Part II
GARDENS AND FLOWERS

Introduction

My love for flowers and gardens has brought me close to many wonderful people, and has enriched my life in other ways as well. I must admit right out that I am not a dirt gardener and have no inclination to get on my knees and weed or transplant. But neither am I an armchair gardener. As my friends know, I take gardening seriously and am in close touch with all gardening activities at the restaurants. I often supervise flower and garden maintenance at Kinsale, and, in my enthusiasm to perfect the plantings at Sky High, I'm afraid I'm often in the way of the men who come down from the Westchester Candlelight greenhouses to work for me.

I enjoy reading gardening books and am fascinated by the garden catalogues with their enticing offers of beautiful flowers. I have made serious studies of several plant families—in fact, it was a study of orchids that led me to collecting. I regret I have never had the time to study horticulture formally. However, if experience is the best teacher, I should be promoted to the head of the class. I have been a practical gardener for close to twelve years, and my experience with plants and flowers has spanned my lifetime—from Newfoundland to southern Florida. One thing is certain: I am not a dilettante. For me, plants and flowers are not an escape from the cares of the day. On the contrary, they sometimes contribute to them. For me, there is no such thing as "carefree" gardening. But I am just as drawn to flowers now as I was as a child gathering potato blossoms, or as a young girl tenderly bringing bouquets of daffodils home to my room in Brooklyn.

I hope that non-gardening readers will remember that it is not pride of possession that compels gardeners to talk or write about their flowers, but a desire to share with others the beauty embodied in gardening.

Let me begin my garden story by revealing my great distaste for arranging flowers in a tortured and unnatural way. I suspect my prejudice against such arrangements began as a girl, when I bought daffodils that seemed to be crying for release from the string with which the florist bound them so tightly in bunches. I like to see flowers casually placed in a vase in the manner of Matisse, Cézanne, or Van Gogh; or to see them arranged as the Japanese do it, so that one is unmindful in viewing them that they have been taken from a garden. A few flowers, even one perfect one, will make my spirits soar and be equally as delightful to me as an exuberant mixture in an important bouquet.

I can't bear to see cut flowers which are not in an ample amount of water; even the orchid corsages on sale in our greenhouses are made in a tiny vial containing a spongelike substance that holds moisture and keeps them fresh. Just as I like to see cut flowers that look happy in a vase, I like to see plants and flowers growing in surroundings that complement them and allow them to enjoy good health. It is painful for me to see a rhododendron which loves acid soil, struggling for life in a limestone area, or to see the leaves of an orchid that prefers shade turning deep green because they are getting too much sun.

When friends visiting me for the first time at Kinsale ask which of the gardens there I prefer—the formal, informal, or naturalistic (a term that has lost favor among landscape architects)—I have to admit that I have no preference in garden styles. Usually, however, small gardens, like the quiet gardens at Kinsale, the orchid glen at Bahia Mar, and the tropical garden at Westchester, are to me the most enchanting.

The style of a garden is determined by the terrain, the architecture of the house it is to accompany, and the mood the gardener wants to evoke. On a large setting, like Kinsale, or the Westchester and Bahia Mar restaurants, it is quite possible to combine all three styles in a single landscape composition, extending for acres. Of course, one of the greatest joys of gardening is that no two gardens are alike; each has a character all its own.

Through the years I have discovered that an interest in gardening takes you well beyond your own garden wall. It brings you in touch with people who have interests similar to your own. This has, for me, resulted in many friendships with professional garden people, including scientists in many fields that are related to horticulture. Although I am probably the most garden-minded hostess in New York, I had a disquieting moment at a party not long ago when out of the corner of my eye I saw a prominent entomologist from one of the botanical gardens furtively examining some of my house plants for signs of insect damage.

Gardening has also added new dimensions to my travels. It heightens my interest in the natural landscape and, when I am in search of historic gardens, it takes me on byways I would otherwise miss. When you stop the car to examine a wilding, you have time to appreciate the countryside more fully. If you are in a buying mood, there are usually noteworthy nurseries to visit, where you find unusual plants to ship or take home to your garden. And on travels abroad and in America, my interest in gardening has brought me to some of the most lovely places, and has given me an opportunity to meet many charming people and, in turn, to invite them to my gardens.

I am concerned about the future of professional gardening in America, and, for that matter, in Europe, too. Through no fault of theirs, young people are turning from gardening as a career and even as a hobby. Curiously enough, I became most aware of this in Ireland a few summers ago when my mother and I were staying in an old castle. The owners, from whom I had rented it, explained that they were able to keep up the two-hundred-year-old lawn, which was lovely, but apologized for the gardens, which were in only fair condition because it was impossible to find enough trained gardeners to tend them properly.

With the passing of great estates, the challenge in horticulture has shifted to the average homeowner. The future of American gardening rests in suburban backyards. And it pleases me that many young homeowners get the inspiration to plant a garden of their own after visiting my gardens.

SOME OF THE
MANY AWARDS
AND CITATIONS
FOR
HORTICULTURE
PRESENTED TO
MISS MURPHY

ARRANGEMENT OF ORCHIDS AWARDED FIRST PRIZE, INTERNATIONAL FLOWER SHOW, NEW YORK, 1961

ARRANGEMENT OF BEGONIAS AWARDED THE TROPHY OF THE HORTICULTURE SOCIETY OF NEW YORK, 1961

CHAPTER ONE

GARDEN FIFTEEN FLOORS UP

MY LATEST VENTURES in gardening are the plantings on the terraces that surround Sky High. From each room, I look out on flowers carefully selected to blend with the interior color schemes. There are chrysanthemums in fall—bronze and yellow ones to heighten the gold motif of the living room, and lustrous pink ones to harmonize with my pink bedroom. In spring there are tulips, daffodils, azaleas, and primroses brought to New York from the greenhouses at Westchester. In summer there is a blaze of color from petunias and other annual flowers, the petunias cascading down the front of the brick walls that contain the soil in the raised planting beds.

Last summer, guests were intrigued by the new climbing strawberry named Sonjana, whose growth I carefully guided on trellises provided for them. Wind is a problem when you garden fifteen floors in the air. And it is not only hard on climbing plants, but on the lantanas, fuchsias, and geraniums trained as little trees and used as accents at the corners of the major plantings.

There are permanent plants on the terraces in addition to the seasonal flowers I have just mentioned. A year-round rose garden of hybrid teas and tree roses is directly opposite my study window, and an herb garden keeps the kitchen stocked with fresh chives, parsley, and sage. Evergreen hedges of boxleaf holly and yews, plus tall California privet (which thrives in spite of cold winter winds), make deep green backgrounds for most of the floral displays. And there are weeping willow trees and tall hemlocks in gigantic tubs in the protected corners of the building. They give needed height to the plantings and allow me to display attractively several pieces of Italian sculpture.

My special joy is the tropical planting just outside the French doors through which you enter the terrace gardens. This planting is set out in early summer, some of the tubbed plants, like the gray-leaved, pink-flowered oleanders, having been brought to New York from Kinsale. This portion of the terrace, on which there are chairs and tables for dining, is covered with a green glass awning that protects the tropical plants from heavy rains, but admits enough light for orchids, hibiscus, crotons, and many foliage plants to grow well. A pool with a tiny waterfall is surrounded by bird-of-paradise flowers, Hawaiian ti plants, luxuriant African violets, and a collection of unusual begonias. I am most proud of these last, for they won the New York Horticultural Society Trophy and the Gold Medal at the International Flower Show in the New York Coliseum in 1958.

When, in late September, the nights become too cool for tropical plantings, they are returned to the greenhouses, and potted chrysanthemums are carried up in the elevators and set out in the planting beds. At Thanksgiving the terrace takes on a festive country air, with cornstalks, pumpkins, and branches of colorful oak leaves banked behind the chrysanthemums. Then, for Christmas, tubbed spruce trees in assorted sizes are arranged on the terrace to create the illusion of a forest in miniature. At night each tree sparkles with tiny lights, similar to those we use in decorations at the restaurants.

Just as at the restaurants or at Kinsale, plantings are not confined to the outdoors. There is a long planter of philodendrons and caladiums in a skylighted passage between the foyer and my study, and tall scheffleras and podocarpus in tubs on either side of the French doors also heighten the indoor-outdoor effect. Cypripedium orchids are set at the base of these tropical trees for an added color note. With a greenhouse to draw upon, I find it difficult, as you can see, to restrain myself in the use of plants and flowers in my New York home.

On the coffee table I have either a simple crystal vase of tall flowers—orange-red dahlias, perhaps the lovely carnation called Tangerine—or a pot-grown cattleya orchid in full flower as the floral accent for the living room. On the desk in my study and on my dressing table there is always at least one perfect flower, for it is not necessary to have a big, important bouquet to make a room delightful.

At Christmas one of my favorite decorations is a great bowl of green cypripedium orchids and variegated holly leaves on the buffet. I have a passion for combining pink and red sweetheart roses for Christmas party tables, with perhaps a few artificial birds—particularly red cardinals—for added interest. In the octagonal hall just off the dining room there are niches in which little formal trees are placed. They are the exception to my rule for never employing flowers in a stylized manner. At Christmas the trees may be made of boxwood and red roses, while at Thanksgiving they may be of fruit—miniatures of the gigantic fruit trees featured at each of the restaurants.

Flowers are for sharing, and I was thrilled last Christmas when the *New York Times* photographed Sky High's decorations for a special feature, and delighted when a group of professional interior decorators called in the spring to see rooms in which plants and flowers are dominant. Regrettably, I could not be on hand to greet them personally. Few people realize how many things there are to do in running two restaurants, and I do not know the luxury of much free time.

Chapter Two

ESTATE IN PORT SEWALL

There was no rhyme or reason to the plantings at Kinsale when we acquired it. Apparently the former owner pointed with a walking stick to a location for each tree and shrub. To my mind the effect was chaos, although there were a few fine big lawn trees, a young citrus grove, and a line of melalucas on either side of the drive for which to be thankful.

But the land (over forty-eight acres in all), a sort of promontory jutting into the water, is a commanding location on Florida's east coast, rising twenty-five feet or so above sea level. We saw at once it had great landscape possibilities.

As the remodeling of the house began we enlisted the help of Boynton Landscape Company of Palm Beach in locating terraces, gardens, pools and the like, for a house and garden must be planned as a unit if they are to get on happily together. George Spencer and Thomas Rawls, two of the firm's landscape architects, were most understanding of our needs, and the garden complex took shape on paper. Today, formal and informal plantings meet at Kinsale, and the contrast between them makes for excitement.

Gardens don't just happen overnight, not even in Florida where you can almost see plants growing. From November through January each year there is a great surge of planting as new trees and large shrubs discovered on tours of the countryside arrive on the nursery trucks, and crews of workers move existing trees to more advantageous locations as prescribed by plan. Garden construction is saved for the summer months, when tree planting is not always so successful. The terrace in front of the living room, looking directly into the view, the sheltered patio by the garden room, the pool and cabana designed by Captain Kiernan, and finally the orchid houses and the vegetable garden were built in about that sequence over the years.

Captain Kiernan and I had visited many of the famous gardens of Europe and America long before Kinsale became a reality. It should have been a simple matter to give the Boynton Nursery people a very specific idea of how we wanted Kinsale's grounds to look. But if you have ever tried to decide where to place a flower border or terrace, you know such decisions are not easy in spite of the fact that you have seen dozens of good flower borders and had tea on some of the most handsome terraces.

What we did was outline our needs, practical and esthetic. We walked over the property hundreds of times studying it at various hours of the day, for light and shadow play a great part in landscape design. A tree that seems to contribute little beauty at mid-day may be extremely exciting to see in the evening, etched against the fading sun or lighted by flares or spotlights.

Groups of trees and shrubs, varieties that we especially liked, were earmarked for saving if at all possible in the final plan. Views of water features and terraces had to be decided, and even such minute details as my preferences for the color of gravel in paths were considered at great length. On trips North

I had time to think out each proposal and study tentative plans as they rolled from the drawing boards. George and Tom were determined that the gardens at Kinsale would definitely be "me," and now that the gardens are real, I think all of us agree we made a perfect team. Tom continues to supervise the maintenance for me, and his watchful eye keeps everything as it should be.

Florida gardening became a real challenge. I was intrigued by lush tropical growth and its accompaniment of gorgeous colorful blooms, but I couldn't imagine a garden without the flowers I knew up North. I read books, pamphlets, and anything else I could lay my hands on pertaining to Florida horticulture. I discovered that many of the flowers conceded to be "impossible" in Florida had been grown successfully here at one time or other. I was determined to have them and experiment with others as well. Tom entered enthusiastically into the many experiments I proposed, and today, as a matter of course, we have roses, delphiniums, snapdragons, hollyhocks (a spellbinding bed of them in front of the fanlike growth of a traveler's palm) and of course tulips, daffodils, and many other plants unusual for Florida. The flora of tropics and temperate zone meet face to face at Kinsale and grow with abandon.

In addition to having plants of the North at Kinsale, I wanted the gardens to be in tune with the natural landscape, particularly the landscape just west of Kinsale, which was so delightfully described by Marjorie Kinnan Rawlings in *The Yearling*. No one can duplicate nature, but we have two utterly charming gardens whose exuberant tropical vegetation certainly captures at least the spirit of nature.

One of them I have come to call the quiet garden; its paths of green zoysia grass are so restful to wander on as they gently curve down the slope to one side of the swimming pool and cabana. You stroll in silence created by the density of tree ferns, tall palms, and trees on whose branches orchids and bromeliads have taken hold. In a clearing that comes as a surprise at the end of one path is a statue of Saint Jude, the patron saint of the impossible.

Natural-looking outcrops of coral rock imported from miles away lend their subtle orange-tan tones as contrast to the lush green and metallic grays of the succulents planted between them. Self-heading philodendrons, which I cannot recommend too highly for Florida gardeners, contribute greatly to the tropical setting. And the blue ginger collected on one of my trips to Hawaii is a dream, although it must be coaxed into flower in Florida.

The other natural garden is reached through the orchid lath house and the greenhouses at the foot of the drive through which you also gain access to the vegetable garden. It is completely secluded in a sort of man-made valley, and in its center is a circular pool fed by natural springs and an artesian well from which we obtain irrigation water for the orchid collections and vegetables. For a long time, the perfect shape of the pool disturbed me, for although it is charming, what with grass on the slopes all around it, I hadn't thought nature was so geometrical. Then not long ago, flying in my plane over North Carolina, not far from Wilmington, I looked down and there was a big perfectly oval natural lake. My qualms about our circular natural pool were dispelled. Coconut palms, Alexander palms, erica palms, all contrasted against sea-grapes—that marvelously adaptable wild tree with its beautifully shiny round leaves—and the evergreen auricaria trees with ledgelike branches in circles around the trunks, are among the plants that give this wild garden its distinctive charm. Completing the picture, of course, is a fountain playing constantly on the water's surface.

One of the fascinating sights, I think, is in complete contrast to the natural gardens. It is the radial rose and cutting garden carved into the orange grove to the left of the drive. It is enclosed by a trim, sheared, four-foot hedge of Ficus nitida, an excellent hedge plant that gardeners new to Florida should come to know at once. As you enter the garden you look across the rose beds and the central bed of white calla lilies at the traveler's palm opposite—a perfect example of natural sculpture. Roses are featured, of course, and they take a bit of doing from central Florida southward. Although it is possible to keep them growing for several years, they never get a good rest as they do during the winter up North, and therefore they bloom themselves to death. I have found it more practical to set out new bare-root plants each October, obtaining them from Texas or California nurseries. Spaced twelve to fifteen inches apart, floribundias and hybrid teas grow side by side in the beds. They begin to flower in early January, reaching full bloom by February and continuing until summer. Pink is my favorite color, and over the past years we have grown almost every pink rose you can think of on a one-year basis.

Pink Pinocchio and Red Garnette do splendidly and are apparently the exception to the rule, for several neighbors have plants that have flowered constantly for years with little care. However, they must allow these plants to grow very tall, and, of course, tall plants would destroy the pattern effect I so dearly love not only at Kinsale but at the Westchester and Bahia Mar restaurants as well.

Peatmoss, rotted manure, and compost are worked deeply into the rose beds before each planting, and the plants are fed with a water-soluble fertilizer each month. Foliar feeding has proved most satisfactory. They are sprayed with all-purpose insecticide-fungicides almost weekly, and the only pruning they need comes when we cut flowers for bud vases to accompany breakfast trays for guests and for lavish, unstudied arrangements everywhere.

Annuals and perennials grown as annuals are set out in great informal drifts in the continuous border that circles the rose garden backed by the ficus hedge. Sweet alyssum, verbena, candy-tuft, ageratum, pansies, globe amaranth, stocks, strawflowers, delphinium, larkspur, and lupins are among those that do splendidly in Florida during the winter. They, like the hollyhocks, are started from seed, the seedlings transplanted to flats and held in a lath house until December when the young plants are set outdoors. Many flats of these plants find their way to the Bahia Mar restaurant gardens to the nostalgic delight of northerners wintering or living permanently in Fort Lauderdale. Flowering begins in late January and continues until the sun gets really hot in early summer.

At Westchester and Bahia Mar we are always looking for more garden space, but at Kinsale we have all we need, although land is costly to reclaim, choked by Australian pines and scrubby palms. Our vegetable garden is on a swamp filled in with muck and marl worth its weight in gold. It is a rectangle some 150 feet across and about 200 feet long. A wide grass path, bordered with parsley, cuts down its center, and the rows of vegetables are planted in raised earth beds that insure good drainage.

You enter the vegetable garden through the orchid house or its adjoining terrace, the terrace being enclosed with pink-flowering Euphorbia fulgens trained as a hedge. Broad steps from the terrace to the path make the descent easy, and you look the length of the garden to the white potting shed flanked on either side by a long white arbor covered with bright vines, including a splendid datura.

The vegetables are grown for the house, our neighbors, and my mother who has a flower garden of her own at Fort Lauderdale. The excess harvest is sent to Bahia Mar, although I don't say too much about this, for we can't supply all the vegetables we need there. Our crop is quite varied. Victor wants Chinese bitter melons, for which I couldn't care less. I want pineapples, he wants papayas—so we have them all.

The pineapples—symbols of hospitality—are dear little plants when you set them out, and just eighteen months later, they produce huge fruit that is nothing at all like the ones that come into market from South America.

The melons are superb, too. One of the boys, who is quite regular in his work, cuts a sort of cross in some of them, and they grow bigger and are tastier than all the others. Or so I'm told, for somehow or other they never reach the house.

Many of the vegetables are planted at fourteen-day intervals all winter, so we have a continuous harvest, starting about November and continuing until late May or early June. Besides pineapples and melons, we have radishes, carrots, turnips, endive, cabbage, onions, lettuce of many kinds, peppers, beets, tomatoes, squash, cucumbers, broccoli, snap beans, and corn. Strawberries do splendidly, mulched heavily and grown on organically enriched soil.

Soil in Florida is a real problem. Each year it must be enriched with manure and its texture improved with compost and peatmoss. All our citrus trees are mulched with peatmoss, which seems to keep their roots cool and the trees growing productively. The soil in the vegetable garden is fumigated each year several weeks before planting to control nematodes, soil-borne diseases, and to kill weed seeds—especially those of nut grass, which is impossible, we find, to eradicate completely. It plagues the gardeners as well as the fumigant manufacturer, who has sent representatives on special trips to Kinsale to see what can be done about it.

To northerners many of the garden practices at Kinsale must seem commonplace, but many of them are quite new to Florida. People from the state experiment station, commercial growers, and experienced amateur plantsmen often honor us by dropping by to see what we are doing and have done. Everyone has come to expect the unusual at Kinsale, for we have been breaking traditional Florida gardening rules ever since the day we moved in.

Tulips in flower in mid-February proved to be a great surprise for all—orchids and tulips side by side; can you imagine the effect? The Associated Bulb Growers of Holland were especially interested in this project, as was the National Tulip Society. For our first planting, we obtained bulbs directly from Holland and pre-cooled them in a refrigerator before planting. They weren't a brilliant success. So the following November, when the bulbs in the tulip displays at Westchester were dug, Victor carefully stored them in an unheated but well-ventilated shed until January. They were then crated, shipped to Kinsale, and planted in a long bed near the orchid lath house where the soil is quite sandy. They were absolutely lovely in full flower in mid-February and continued to bloom according to variety until March. Everyone came from miles around to see them, and each year we repeat the display, 5,000 tulip bulbs!

We find it is best to set the bulbs just two inches beneath the soil surface and space them not more than four inches apart. The first leaves appear above ground ten to fifteen days after planting. The single varieties do best; the parrot types are not too satisfactory. Daffodils, planted at the same time and also pre-cooled at Westchester, show above ground a month after planting and flower just ahead of the earliest tulips—their natural sequence. Paperwhite narcissus, planted with the daffodils and tulips, come up and flower just two weeks after planting, and lily-of-the-valley from pre-cooled pips add their lovely fragrance to the display.

Horticultural challenges like these keep us on our toes at Kinsale and make gardening interesting, just as the collection of botanical orchids does up North.

Some of the other plants we grow at Kinsale are interesting horticulturally, too. We have Chinese rice plants, so popular on the West Coast, massed in a planting that separates the driveway turncourt in front of the house from the swimming pool. Shortly we will have some of the largest Australian tree ferns in Florida. They are considered quite difficult to grow in these parts, but already it is possible to walk beneath their fronds, which overhang a path in the quiet garden.

Camellias of the japonica type grow not in tubs but in the ground. Easter lilies set in the garden for an April display three years ago have come up and flowered every year since. We have azaleas that bloom quite well year after year, one of my favorites being the lovely pink Coral Bells. Angelwing begonias are usually grown as an annual in this part of Florida, but ours have remained for years, their shiny leaves a wonderful contrast to Boston ferns that have become naturalized under the trees in the natural gardens.

The little bird sanctuary that you look down into from the garden room windows has delightful combination plantings of blue browalias, Christmas or melior begonias, and great mats of pink and blue African violets. The latter seem completely oblivious to the frequent torrential rains of Florida. Who said their leaves must never be sprinkled? We have tried tuberous begonias in this shaded and sheltered nook, but for some unknown reason they don't do well at all.

The plant inventory is too long for a single chapter, but I must mention two long rows of sweetpeas that we plant to climb on chicken wire in the vegetable garden. It is a splendid multicolored variety from Castle MacGarrett, County Mayo, Ireland. The seed is sent to me each year by a dear friend, Lord Oranmore and Browne. And I am very happy about the night-blooming cereus that at first had to be coddled along but is now determined to reach the top of a palm, blooming each year as it goes.

CHAPTER THREE

WESTCHESTER CANDLELIGHT GARDENS

IN ADDITION TO seasonal flower displays indoors and out, we have gardens big and small, gardens to please everyone and to be enjoyed throughout the year at the Westchester Candlelight Restaurant.

There are hundreds of roses, thousands of tulips. There is a lake spanned by a moon bridge which reflects feathery weeping willow trees, and flowering dogwoods and cherries—pink, red, and white in spring. There are masses of pink and white azaleas, and all kinds of flowering shrubs. There is a tropical garden in which orchids and other tropical flowers are set out each summer. In the display greenhouse you see citrus trees in fruit and flower, banana palms, African violets, many rare begonias, tropical hibiscus, gardenias, camellias, and others too numerous to mention. In back of the restaurant, paths wind among the flowers on a floral hillside. A terrace is fringed with rose beds edged with boxwood, and there is a radial garden that glows each spring with tulips. It is centered by a pool. Seasonal displays greet one in the lobby, there are planters filled with blooms in the dining rooms, and there are even baskets of flowers hanging from the ceiling. At one garden entrance the Patricia Murphy Dahlia, a big orange-red decorative flower featured in *LIFE* magazine in color, is displayed each fall. It was named after me by the famous American dahlia hybridizer, Albert Parrella.

The story of the gardens at Westchester begins in 1954, many months before the restaurant was built. There wasn't a trace of the nursery we were told once occupied the site; there was just a barren hillside, a dank swamp, a weedy thistle-grown field. I thought of all the splendid gardens I had ever seen and wondered if any of them had started life as humbly as ours.

With his usual calm determination, Captain Kiernan tackled the job of transforming the site. His knowledge of engineering and his skill in bringing the right people together to accomplish a task came into play at once. The swamp was drained to form the lake; the hillside, shored up with heavy boulders, was reshaped to accommodate the buildings. We suddenly found ourselves in the midst of garden-making on a grand scale. I was a bit frightened.

How to convey the picture I had in mind to a landscape architect posed a problem. Ours was to be, and is, a garden for people—hundreds of people at one time. It had to be spacious, yet give a feeling of intimacy. Color was a paramount need, second only to having as wide an assortment of flowers as possible, for we hoped everyone would find in our garden something that spoke particularly to him. Actually, I wanted a hybrid between a botanical garden and a floral stage setting, and I doubt if a professional designer before or since has been faced with such a challenge. I was fortunate in discovering a designer who speaks my language. He is Edmond Motyka, who has a feeling for flowers and planting combinations that those who have seen our displays must agree is beyond compare.

Knowing how the site for our gardens once looked, you can imagine my delighted surprise when in March, 1956, I received a Citation Award from The Federated Garden Clubs of New York State for accomplishing the greatest improvement in a piece of property in New York State within the year. When I learned that I was to be so honored, I knew the occasion called for a pink champagne party followed by a gold and pink luncheon at which pink roses were featured. Five hundred club members attended, and during the presentation ceremony, I wondered if anyone could imagine that the transformation from weeds to flowers on the hillside alone had cost close to $170,000.

Almost all the flowers you see in the dining rooms, in the seasonal display gardens, and on sale in the display greenhouses we grow ourselves. It requires about twenty men the year round to care for the gardens and for the greenhouses several miles away from the restaurant, where part of the orchid collection is housed. But the gardening staff must be doubled in the fall when the tulip bulbs arrive from Holland to be planted, when the Christmas decorations are put up, and during the summer when maintenance is a constant chore.

Garden-keeping calls for endless planning. I have long conferences with Victor, who is responsible for all the gardens and greenhouses, to decide such things as what seeds or bulbs to order, what new varieties of roses to try. Mary Fitzgerald, who is in charge of the display greenhouses next to the restaurant, is consulted about the flowers she will need, perhaps months hence, for centerpieces, brides' bouquets, corsages, and for seasonal decorative items. She is a genius at flower arranging, never torturing flowers, but arranging them with great taste.

The three of us must be ready at a moment's notice to revise our plans in order to meet the challenge of unseasonable weather. If the roses are slow to bloom because of a cool spell, we must be prepared to set out quantities of flowering annuals for an immediate color effect. Our patrons expect this of us.

A heavy frost last year could have ruined our chrysanthemum display for Thanksgiving, but all the tablecloths we could muster were used to blanket the beds from cold, and our Thanksgiving show went on as scheduled. The gardener's lament, "You should have seen the garden last week when such-and-such was in flower," is not for us.

The most sensational seasonal display, many of our patrons tell us, is the tulip and daffodil planting in the spring. It earned us an International Tulip Award presented personally to me by a sweet little Dutch girl who spoke beautiful English. She was on a goodwill tour of this country, representing Queen Juliana and the Associated Bulb Growers of Holland. She told me that Americans are among the biggest buyers of tulip bulbs in the world, and this speaks well, I think, for our love of flowers. In 1956 the National Tulip Society awarded us its Certificate of Merit "for distinguished public service in providing the most outstanding tulip garden in Westchester."

We obtain 50,000 tulip bulbs each fall, planting them in natural drifts around the lake and on the floral hillside. They are also set out formally row upon row in the radial garden. Some are planted in pots, overwintered in a cold frame, and then brought inside in late February and early March as a preview of spring.

Thousands of daffodils have been naturalized in the gardens, including the lovely varieties, Mount Hood and King Alfred. They are followed by the early-flowering Darwin Hybrid tulips around the lake, and then the main tulip show gets under way with cottage and Darwin types predominating. They are always at their best on Mother's Day. Spring-flowering shrubs provide a floral accompaniment to the tulips and daffodils, and everywhere cherries and flowering dogwoods are a blaze of color.

In late fall, after the spring-flowering bulbs are safely in the soil, the beds are covered with evergreen boughs. The boughs keep the beds attractive during the winter and also keep people from walking on them. After they flower in spring, the bulbs are taken up immediately and 5,000 or so are saved for shipping to Kinsale in January, having been pre-cooled in open sheds. Tulips that have flowered once at Westchester do better in Florida, we find, than new pre-cooled bulbs direct from Holland, even though we can't allow their leaves to mature after flowering. In home gardens, tulips remain in the ground and flower well for two or three springs, possibly longer; but for our purpose we like fresh, vigorous bulbs that are certain to put on a truly lavish display.

Our roses are equally as popular as the tulips. We grow practically all the award-winning All-America Rose Selection varieties in addition to hundreds of others. At the moment I'm closely watching the progress of some rose garlands being trained on the bridge across the lake. I hope they will be as lovely as those at the International Rose Test Garden in Geneva, Switzerland, which intrigued me so on my last trip abroad.

The first surge of color from roses comes in June, and by having plantings of floribundas, grandifloras, and everblooming climbers, we have roses in flower all summer and well into fall.

Rose fanciers will appreciate knowing that long canes of hybrid teas in the formal gardens are shortened to eighteen inches when the bushes are mounded with soil for the winter. In spring, after the soil mound is removed, the men prune hard, leaving as a rule only eight- to twelve-inch canes. In this way we avoid top-heavy plants with flowers so high you can't examine them in detail.

Garden clubs, many from distant states, make pilgrimages to the gardens and lunch with us frequently. Their members are extremely interested in daylilies, which hybridizers have been improving so remarkably, and we now have some well-established plants of the latest varieties in the perennial borders at the base of the hill—borders which are not unlike those found in England. Poppies, Japanese iris, Madonna and rubrum lilies are among the other flowers found there.

Annual flowers dominate the scene in summer. Beds of Unwin and Coltness dahlias, carpets and edgings of sweet alyssum and all kinds of marigolds and zinnias take over when the tulips in the formal beds are lifted. The 1961 All-America Selection petunia, Coral Satin, gets top billing on the pink hill, which is seen as you approach the entrance, where there must always be a lovely glow of pink. All of our annuals are started from seed in the greenhouses in March, painstakingly transplanted to flats, and moved, usually in full bloom, to their garden locations after the last frost in spring.

Discerning gardeners are enthralled by our espaliered firethorns, by tubbed Hinoki cypresses, and by red-berried cotoneasters that cascade down the hillside, brightening it even on the dullest day in winter. No one can help but admire the Japanese maples, their leaves a vivid red and gold in fall, contrasting with the deep green needles of white pines. And everyone is enchanted by the great copper beech tree that Catherin Brun, a specialist in tree finding and moving, discovered for our terrace on an old Connecticut estate. It was she who supervised the heavy construction work on the gardens, work for which she is noted all over the country.

Christmas is the most spectacular season of the year at both Candlelight Restaurants, and it takes weeks to set up the indoor and outdoor displays. The pleasant task of working out new ideas for Christmas often begins in hot July. To be sure, there are all kinds of spangles, stylized and old-fashioned Christmas trees, pine roping, and fragrant wreaths of balsam. But to my mind, living flowers convey the message of Christmas best, and for them we must plan in advance.

Poinsettias are our specialty at the holidays. We know after years of practice how many stock plants are needed to get enough rooted cuttings for exactly the quantity of pot plants we need to give each dining room a glow of red, pink, and white. Deep pink kalanchoes, white and pink cyclamens, and red and white azaleas must also be worked into the Christmas greenhouse planting schedule.

Outside, the crèche and carousel are set up; people look forward to them each year. Evergreen trees and even deciduous ones are bedecked with lights and ornaments. White branches are inserted in the beds and borders to create the illusion of a white Christmas.

While much of our attention is focused on Christmas planning, January's indoor displays of white azaleas must be grown for months ahead of time. April sees our Easter display of fragrant white lilies, and we must prepare 6,000 chrysanthemum plants for Thanksgiving. You may be sure there is always something to be done in the greenhouses. Of course, we find time to enter flower shows, and the greenhouse men share my pride in the hundred or so prizes awarded to us over the years for horticultural entries in shows large and small.

Chapter Four

GARDENS AT BAHIA MAR

The Bahia Mar Restaurant is situated at the end of a pier, and when I first saw it in 1959 I named it the "SS Concrete." With the exception of a few scrubby shrubs and two large trees, which later had to be moved, the building was surrounded by concrete, and the sun shone hot off it as it does off the deck of a ship. There is no concrete now. Just three months after taking over the restaurant, the gardens were completed. I anticipated spending about $35,000 in garden making, so you can imagine my shock when the first bill for $74,900 arrived. But the gardens are perfect gems in a setting of blue, and their cost is all but forgotten. They were designed with the help of the Boynton Landscape Company, which assisted us at Kinsale.

I knew the gardens were a hit just hours after we opened them to the public. Some Dutch sailors off a ship at anchor nearby came in, their faces brightening in the spontaneous way European faces do in appreciation of a lovely garden. Of course, Americans also fell in love with the gardens, and for weeks after we opened, over a hundred people an hour were clocked through the outside garden gate which we put up to divert traffic from the main dining rooms. The popularity of the gardens continues. In fact they have become an institution at Fort Lauderdale; people come from miles around to see them and dine with us. The crowds are not so great, though, that you can't get a long view of the colorful plantings; and you can take time to examine the delicate flowers and photograph them at leisure.

A pattern garden dominates the scene, its beds of flowers as intricate in design as any found at Versailles, where pattern or parterre gardening reached its zenith. We change the flowers in pattern gardens to fit the season.

Christmas is poinsettia time, just as it is in our restaurant in Westchester. To be sure, we also have hundreds of other plants in full bloom then, but poinsettias, 10,000 plants in all, steal the Christmas show. Growing in pots and spaced close together in a wide border along the long window wall, they provide a bright red foreground for the entire garden and the distant marina. Pink and white varieties fill the flower beds to overflowing, and the crowning glory is a raised bed in the center of the garden in which a new double pink poinsettia named Sophia is featured. I am overjoyed, for we have enough plants of it now to begin propagating it in quantity. During this season, which for us begins the middle of December and lasts until mid-January, poinsettias are displayed in the restaurant as well.

The pattern garden is changed completely by the end of March. Where previously poinsettias grew, hundreds of pink and white azaleas from Kinsale and thousands of tulips from Westchester are set out to herald spring. Pink-blossomed peach trees, flowering cherries, and yellow forsythia add a stunning note to the spring show. All are carefully forced into flower at the greenhouses in Westchester and trucked or flown to Bahia Mar for the occasion.

By Easter, the pattern garden undergoes a third transformation—this time into pink, blue, and white hydrangeas and beds of fragrant Easter lilies. They bloom until early summer, when green and white caladiums and sprightly orange and yellow marigolds are set out, all grown, of course, in the greenhouses and lath house at Kinsale.

September sees the first of our two major chrysanthemum plantings. Yellow, gold, and bronze dominate the scene, but lovely pink varieties are included to please me. There are curious spoon and spider types, endearing little pompons, and large types as well. The chrysanthemum displays bring us back to poinsettias, and the seasonal changes at Bahia Mar have run their colorful course.

The showy pattern garden is not all there is to see at Bahia Mar, however. Adjoining it is a rose garden which is constantly in flower, and an Oriental garden complete with a Japanese zigzag bridge that spans a stream and pool, in which a waterfall splashes. There is a long hibiscus walk lined with eighty-four choice varieties. And there is an orchid glen where the most sumptuous specimens in my collection are put on display as soon as they reach flowering perfection. The diversity of gardens at Bahia Mar may not be as great as it is in Westchester, but the gardens are perhaps made more colorful with the help of the tropical climate, which is so conducive to plant growth.

The rose garden is worthy of special mention not only because it is fragrant and colorful, but because rose growing in Florida is, as I have mentioned, a difficult feat. The garden consists of a long central panel of pink and white floribundas, outlined by a low hedge of Euphorbia fulgens that chaperones the roses while reminding visitors to stay on the path. Separated from the central panel by a broad path is a bed of hybrid teas, backed by and set off against an informal hedge of tropical shrubs. In all, we have more rose bushes at Bahia Mar than you could find in all of Broward County, in which Fort Lauderdale is located.

The relatively new pink hybrid tea Peace is a great favorite of mine. Many of the largest blooms find their way to my office above the restaurant, and some are always presented to my mother when she takes dinner with us at Bahia Mar. Some of the Peace blossoms measure six inches across, and Floyd Hopper, who is in charge of garden maintenance at Bahia Mar, is rightfully proud of them. Roses are his special passion and he is experimenting with ways to keep the plants in flower continuously year after year, not changing the plants annually as we do at Kinsale. We shall see. I'm discovering that one can grow almost anything in Florida. Careful records are being kept of all our horticultural practices, and if Floyd meets with the success he anticipates, I hope he will make his rose-growing technique available to all Florida gardeners.

The Oriental gardens, with their pool and waterfall, feature lush tropical vegetation and bizarre and exotic flowers. There are towering bamboos, many kinds of palms, cycads (an early form of plant life, specimens of which we searched far and wide to find), and a big sausage tree that adults as well as children find amusing. There are calla lilies and many bird-of-paradise plants whose splendid orange and blue flowers are a favorite subject for photographers. In addition to the little glen where my orchids are shown, there is a tree whose branches support rare bromeliads, which are related to the pineapple and also to the native red-flowered tillandsias so prevalent in tree branches in the Everglades. Many times I've helped our bromeliads along by pouring tepid water into the funnel their leaves form for water holding.

No one should leave the Oriental gardens without seeing the luxuriant crotons with their curiously shaped and brilliantly colored leaves. Some of them are being propagated by air-layering, which Floridians call "mossing-off," and I will soon have plants of them to take to Westchester for our tropical outdoor summer display.

After dark, spotlights pick up all the colorful flower beds, and little lights by the thousands flicker on and off in the branches of four large sea-grape trees that mark the corners of the pattern garden. At night it almost seems that the gardens are even more fragrant than they are by day.

CHAPTER FIVE

ORCHIDS

OF ALL FLOWERS, orchids are to me the most thrilling. Over the years the collection at Westchester and Kinsale has grown to about 90,000 plants, not including seedlings by the thousands. The major kinds we have are species and varieties of cattleyas, cypripediums, and cymbidiums. But there are less-known genera too, plants the greenhouse boys call "our" botanicals. Some are exceedingly rare and have come to us from such prized collections as Sander's in England and Baldwin's in New York.

Upon opening the show greenhouses at Westchester, I was not surprised that the then modest orchid collection caused great excitement, and everyone wanted to buy orchid corsages. It became imperative to enlarge our collection and produce enough flowers to meet the demand.

Fortunately, an old greenhouse range not far from the restaurant was for sale and I was able to acquire it, along with the nucleus of a commercial orchid collection it contained. Over the years, orchids from this range had gone to New York's most fashionable Park Avenue and Fifth Avenue flower shops to be sold at handsome prices. Today, from the same greenhouses, identical orchids are sold to our restaurant guests for as little as $2.00, and sometimes even less.

My objective is to use the proceeds from orchid sales to pay the salaries of greenhouse men, purchase new plants and seedlings, keep the greenhouses in repair (we did some extensive rebuilding, too), purchase supplies, and pay the fuel bill, which is a major item in the annual $100,000 operating cost of the greenhouse range.

Oddly enough, it was the fuel bill that led to our expanded collection. Most orchids must be grown for several years before they produce flowers, and during this nonproductive period it seemed logical to me to grow the young plants on to flowering size in Florida, where greenhouse heating is rarely needed. I investigated the possibilities, and soon the lovely octagonal lath house at Kinsale, where I had my first orchid collection, began to hum with activity. Young plants filled shelves to overflowing. Eventually, four twenty-foot greenhouses were joined to it, for, as the plants in the lath house began to develop flower buds, I discovered it was safer to bring them into flower in a greenhouse where temperature and humidity can be carefully controlled. Incidentally, one of the greenhouses at Kinsale is air-conditioned, because cypripediums and cymbidiums flower best in a cool temperature that Florida can't often supply.

As all collectors know, it is impossible to stop collecting once you start, and you can imagine that it wasn't long before I needed more space for orchids. I decided to experiment with orchids in a combination greenhouse-lath house made of Saran, a plastic cloth. The house measures 30 x 100 feet, and its roof and cloth sides are supported by a giant wooden frame. Orchids fill its benches and they do splendidly, for the cloth retains the humidity that orchids love, provides filtered light, and keeps out rain which can damage the plants.

Devoted Victor, who, as I have mentioned, supervises the

gardens and greenhouses at Westchester, keeps a watchful eye on orchid growing at Kinsale and coordinates our gardening activities. But with the expansion of the collection came the need for a trained orchid grower to be on hand at all times at Kinsale. I hired Carter Funnell, who has had many years of experience with orchids and is doing a superlative job for me.

Orchid growing on a large scale is an adventure not without hazards. If I am in New York when the weather bureau announces that a freeze is expected in Florida, I cannot wait to pick up a phone and talk with the greenhouse boys at Kinsale. A freeze could wipe out our entire collection. At such times as many plants as possible are moved into the greenhouses, and heaters like those used in citrus groves are set up in the cloth and lath houses. In the Westchester greenhouses we have an alarm that warns of sudden temperature fluctuations so that ventilators can be opened or closed, or the great furnaces turned on if needed.

To walk in the warm moist air of the fragrant show greenhouses at Westchester is a delight to our guests, who little realize the many activities going on behind the scenes. Who would dream that thousands of gallons of insecticides and liquid fertilizers are applied to the plants each year, or that weeks are needed for necessary transplantings. Even the cutting of flowers takes time, for each flower is painstakingly placed in a box and kept cool in a refrigerator to improve its keeping quality.

Cattleyas, the big white orchids most brides cherish on their wedding day, are the most popular orchids we grow. There are about sixty-five known species native to continental tropical America, and many thousands of magnificent hybrids. I can't even estimate the number of different kinds we have. There are those whose sepals and petals are violet or shades and tints of purple, while the labellum, or lip, has definite markings of lighter tints or lines of yellow or white.

Pure white hybrids are especially prized, and markings of yellow and gold add to their richness. Their flowers are borne singly or in clusters, according to the habit of the particular species, while the number of flowers on a plant depends upon its vigor and age. We have had some prize-winning hybrids with as many as twenty flowers, each measuring at least eight inches across.

The cattleyas are for the most part epiphytic orchids, obtaining their food from the air or, where they grow in the wild, from debris that collects in the crevices of tree branches. They are not parasites, as some people think. In cultivation, of course, they are grown in pots, osmunda packed around their roots. More recently, we have been using fir bark as a growing medium and find it most satisfactory.

Our cymbidiums are lovely, too. Their ivory white to deep maroon flowers keep well and resemble cattleyas, although they are smaller. They number ten to twenty or more on sprays two to three feet long. This genus is made up of about seventy species found mostly at high elevations in Asia, Africa, and Australia. They are predominantly terrestrial, growing in soil, and the plants are large, with long, graceful, grassy-looking leaves. We display the plants in full flower in the show greenhouse at Westchester and outdoors at Bahia Mar. The most spectacular always find their way to flower shows in the New York City area and in southern Florida, where they have won various prizes.

Cypripediums are the third genus of orchid we grow on a large scale. They are often called lady's-slippers because of their flower's saclike lips. They, too, are terrestrial, and there are about fifty species, which includes the moccasin flower found in northern woods. Prized for the unusual shape and intricacy of their flower markings, they range from light chartreuse to deep copper, purple, and pink. Some have handsome mottled leaves that make them interesting house plants even when not in bloom. A variety which I particularly like is Cypripedium maudiae, or more correctly in botanical circles, Paphiopedilum maudiae. It has startling white flowers with distinct green stripes. This variety was featured in our orchid exhibit at the last International Flower Show, which was complete with tropical plants of many kinds and a gurgling brook. But it was the orchids, including this—my favorite—which brought us a coveted first prize.

The other orchids we grow are primarily for display in the restaurants, where diners can enjoy them. There are, among others, dendrobium, epidendrum, laelia, laelia-cattleya, miltonia, odontoglossum, odontioda, oncidium, phalaenopsis, and vandas, some of which I imported from Hawaii.

I have had the privilege of obtaining some fine cattleya hybrids which I registered with the Royal Horticultural Society in London, official registrar of orchids. I named a beautiful lavender hybrid for Jean MacArthur, General MacArthur's wife. A deep purple hybrid is called Clementine Paddleford, in honor of the food editor of the *New York Herald Tribune,* who often dines with us. Another purple one is named Susan Wagner after New York City Mayor Wagner's wife.

Late in 1957 I decided to enter a garden class in the New York flower show to be held the following March. It was a new and challenging venture for me, and I asked Ed Motyka, who over the years has staged the seasonal floral displays at the restaurants, to accompany me to Hawaii, where I was to attend the International Orchid Conference. In my free moments we visited many splendid orchid gardens, studying and photographing them in preparation to staging the orchid garden at the forthcoming show. Upon our return we worked over plans, gathered the necessary material, and began an almost daily watch of the progress of the plants being forced into flower at the greenhouses.

Few people viewing a flower show garden realize the amount

of work it represents. Many more plants than will be used must be brought into perfect bloom so one is sure of an ample supply on show day. Their transportation to the show must be scheduled carefully, and capable people found to assist in setting up a show garden—an art quite different from outdoor garden building.

A garden like the one we finally set up had never before been staged at an International Flower Show, not even in the days when great estates entered the show with gardens that were phenomenal horticultural feats, breathtaking in their splendor. Ours was different because it was completely enclosed by a tall camellia hedge. People lined up at the gate to enter it, for it could not be seen from the aisles. It was not a garden merely to be looked at from a distance, but one to be fully experienced by walking among lovely tropical plants, along paths shaded by giant trees on whose branches orchids were placed. Because it was completely enclosed, you felt, upon entering it, far removed from the hectic tempo of the flower show all around. It gave people an excellent opportunity to see how orchids grow in the wild.

The garden was a tremendous success, winning an International Flower Show Trophy and a Horticultural Society of New York Gold Medal. After the show, it was reassembled outdoors at Westchester, where each summer it is planted with tropical plants and orchids. Several camellias from the original show are still there—protected, of course, in winter—and I am as proud of them as I can be. I hope they will survive the subzero weather the gardens at Westchester are experiencing as I write these words about them.

In a commercial exhibit, also in 1958, I introduced my floral perfumes for the first time, and people were as intrigued by them as they were with our tropical orchid garden on the main show floor.

The debut of Patricia Murphy Floral Perfumes was

launched with Green Orchid, Gold Orchid, and Regina Rose (the last named for my husband's niece), which still continue their popularity. In the 1959 International Flower Show we staged an orchid carousel, covered with 2,500 white and 2,500 pink orchids set close together to form a striped awning. Photographs of it appeared in the newspapers, for while it was a commercial exhibit, it still made horticultural news.

Orchids, as you can see, are very much a part of my life. There is almost always a specimen plant on the coffee table at Sky High, where the foyer steps leading to the garden terraces are flanked by chartreuse and purple cypripediums. Potted orchids in full flower last many weeks in the house—sometimes a month or more—and they require less care than a short-lived bouquet of roses or carnations.

Orchids grow in trees on either side of the cabana at Kinsale, and one looks up at them while swimming in the pool.

I suggested to Al Cabana, my pilot, that we install a little vase for orchids beside each seat in the plane, like the ones in elegant old limousines. But he overruled me. Perhaps from a man's point of view he is right, but I don't really think you can overdo with orchids.

Part III

MY FAVORITE FOODS AND MENUS

Introduction

I HAVE WRITTEN in Part I about the fateful evening when I walked down a street in Brooklyn Heights right into my career. Bitterly discouraged, short on funds, and facing the bleak realities of the oncoming depression, I was also plain hungry. But I was not so hungry that I didn't seriously consider spending the thirty-five cents I had allowed myself for dinner on a small bouquet of flowers, so that I could sit in my furnished room, savoring their beauty while fooling my empty insides with dry raisins and several glasses of water.

It is not surprising, then, that in all my efforts to make dining attractive to millions of people, I have always used beautiful flowers to make sitting down at table more than the mere business of eating.

Of course, there are many other attractive accompaniments to satisfying dining. In my restaurants I have tried to give my guests both food and atmosphere they were not likely to have at home, or even in an ordinary restaurant. The candlelight that has featured so prominently in my career has always been glowing from the start, casting a lovely light for relaxed dining, gaiety, and conviviality. Aside from its romantic and elegant connotations, it provides an intimacy that nothing else could achieve in a large dining area. And it is so flattering to the ladies!

Most of my customers like the swirl and excitement of large crowds, for Americans are naturally gregarious, but in catering to groups one must never forget the individual. That is why there are candles. That is why guests are served individual little loaves of bread on little wood carving boards, and why I insist that a birthday or anniversary be serenaded for all to hear.

When it comes to offering people food that they would not bother to prepare at home, I have always been on the lookout for dishes that are different and require some effort in preparation, whether or not they are exotic. The popovers, which have been a sort of Patricia Murphy trade-mark, were not hit upon accidentally. I went through scores of recipes alphabetically for hot breads of every description and decided that this light, air-filled, golden-brown, crusty delicacy was the most attractive of them all and would be best remembered. You will discover in the following pages how to make my popovers, as well as how to prepare many other dishes I serve in my restaurants and homes.

If entertaining is a high art, as I think it should be—in public as well as in the privacy of one's own dining room—then one should approach the preparation and serving of food like a composer or painter. There should be themes and sub-themes in an attractive meal, strong, vital passages mixed with subtle obbligatos. There should always be a sense of harmony, in the surroundings as well as in the succession of courses. Visually, there should be pleasing and relaxing blends of color, in the food itself and in the backgrounds.

There is no excuse for heaping a plate with dull brown and white edibles, all tasting very much alike. We have a wide range of taste sensations, and combinations of these make the range even wider. You will find that my recipes make a special point of contrasts, even in a single dish. And nature has given us enough colors in vegetables, meats, sauces and accompanying condiments or jellies to make any meal a feast for the eye as well as for the inner man.

Color plays a major part in table decorations, too, I think. Petal pink and mint green can be varied with great success, while gold and white is an irresistibly elegant accompaniment

THE WESTCHESTER CANDLELIGHT

THE COLONNADED ATRIUM OF THE BAHIA MAR CANDLELIGHT
FORT LAUDERDALE, FLORIDA

EXTERIOR OF THE BAHIA MAR CANDLELIGHT

to formal dinners. Centerpieces, incidentally, should always be low enough so that diners may see one another and the general atmosphere, not just a huge bouquet in the middle of a table.

The china should frame fine food unostentatiously, but with as much elegant accent as possible. I believe in using everything one has, whether it be an heirloom, an objet d'art, or a workaday mug. Neither in my restaurants nor in my homes do I have a lot of showy, ornamental dishes or glasses which are to be seen but not used. If the food is the best you can serve, it deserves the flattery of lovely containers or backgrounds. Collections are fine in museums, but they don't add anything to a meal sitting vacantly on a shelf or in a cabinet.

In a restaurant one has the chance to carry the scenic design for dining to exciting lengths. Both in Westchester and Bahia Mar I have featured fountains which offer the relaxing sound of running water and the kaleidoscopic glints of splashing streams pinpointed by subtle lighting.

The gardens in both restaurants are easily accessible to those waiting to be seated, for those tarrying after the meal, and for those who, as some do, wander into the restaurants merely to enjoy the shrubs and flowers. My gift shops serve the same purpose—to put people in the mood for leisurely enjoyment of dining. It is a hard thing to achieve in the hurly-burly of modern living. Moreover, lots of people like to buy our own breads, cookies, jellies and jams on sale in the gift shop to liven up a meal at home.

Color plays its part in the costumes of the boys and girls, many hundred strong, who serve Candlelight meals. These colors vary according to the seasons, of course, but they are designed to set off our help to the very best advantage and accent the excitement of a holiday. And let me tell you, the waiters and waitresses love to be dressed handsomely, and I am certain they give a little extra in service knowing that they are elegantly costumed performers on a well-appointed stage.

At Kinsale in Florida and in my New York penthouse, Sky High, I have had the opportunity to keep the backgrounds for dining as flexible as they are at my Candlelights. In Florida, guests may find themselves seated in a spacious dining room, in the cabana with its marble floors, at poolside, or on one of several terraces overlooking the lagoon and the Blooming Island. Out of his fabulous culinary knowledge my chef, Victor, prepares some wonderful dishes, which I am sharing with you for the first time in the Kinsale menus. He also uses great imagination in varying meals for different settings.

At Sky High, one may sit in state in a formal dining room, or gaze at the ever-changing New York skyline as meals are served on one of the terraces. The food I serve in the city is considerably different, of course, from that in semi-tropical Kinsale, as you will discover in browsing through the menus. Here again, I am sharing a number of secrets that I have not even told to my close friends. As in the case of the Candlelight recipes, you will find nothing overpoweringly elaborate or so specialized that it would only fit into the diet of a few gourmets.

Here is a compendium of favorite dishes enjoyed by my public and private guests. You may not find a new way to capture the elusive flavor and savor of a truffle or plover's egg, but I think that you will become acquainted with some favorite dishes of Americans, ordered not once but many, many times by millions of diners over several decades. My chefs were reluctant to give up their secrets, as all good chefs are, but I prevailed upon them to share their wizardry with you.

The menus and recipes are divided into four parts, covering the restaurants and my two homes, because I feel that people tend to associate dishes with the places where they have eaten them. It has been fun making dining a happy event. Bon appétit!

Section One

KINSALE

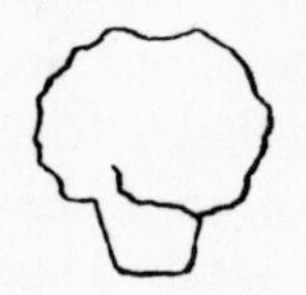

There is something very special about the recipes you will find here, for Kinsale is my own true home. It is where I spent the happiest years of my life with Rosie, and where we entertained in so many varied ways—from having a few friends at table to serving more than four hundred guests at a buffet dinner. There are some surprising concoctions here, but Kinsale, just north of Palm Beach, is a place of surprises. For example, the illusion it creates of a rocky hillside achieved on the flat Florida coast, or the profusion of fruits and vegetables raised in greenhouse and garden to insure fresh ingredients in menus. Such home-grown products are used not only at Kinsale but in the Westchester and Bahia Mar Candlelights, to which they are flown in my busy airplane, "Miss Tango."

All the dishes cited here are prepared and served under the beneficent sign of the pineapple—the 18th century symbol of hospitality—which graces my homes and my restaurants. Therefore, many recipes call for pineapple. The "doctored" watermelon, which I mentioned in the story of my life, is a rather special concoction for special occasions, but I don't see why it needs a yachting expedition to be enjoyed. Victor's great All-White Salad, made of white radishes, sliced apple, grapefruit, and the like, is picturesque in the semi-tropical atmosphere of Kinsale, but, like the champagne-soaked watermelon, it could be a conversation piece in any climate.

Among the recipes that follow are such taste sensations as Chicken Victor with Dumplings and the Duckling Flambé. These are favorites of my closest friends, who will discover for the first time just how they are fashioned. For expansive home entertaining the buffet is ideal. There is no end to the combinations for home entertaining—including the serving of that great hot bread, the popover, which is so important in my life that I wear a gold popover charm on my charm bracelet.

Kinsale would not be Kinsale, of course, without my cherished and devoted major domo, Victor de Leon—a fine chef with an international background. He is a Filipino by birth, but loves to confuse Florida natives by passing himself off as a full-blooded American Indian.

Menu

BUFFET

COCKTAILS

SHRIMP ASPIC CANAPÉS *

HAWAIIAN CHICKEN AND PINEAPPLE CURRY *

CONDIMENTS

(CHUTNEY, RAISINS, COCONUT, PEANUTS, ETC.)

OUR OWN AVOCADO AND GRAPEFRUIT SALAD

FLORIDA KEY LIME PIE *

COFFEE TEA

* recipe follows

SHRIMP ASPIC CANAPÉS

- 1 envelope unflavored gelatine
- 1½ cups chicken broth
- 1 cup Rhine wine
- Dash Tabasco
- ½ teaspoon Worcestershire
- ½ teaspoon salt
- 30 small shrimp, cooked and cleaned
- 30 Melba toast rounds
- Mayonnaise

Soften gelatine in ¼ cup cold chicken broth. Heat remaining broth; add to gelatine, stir until dissolved. Cool; add wine, Tabasco, Worcestershire and salt. Oil 30 tiny muffin cups (1¼-inches bottom diameter). Place 1 shrimp in each. Add just enough gelatine mixture to barely cover shrimp. Chill until firm. Unmold. Spread toast rounds with mayonnaise; top with shrimp in aspic. Makes 30 canapés.

HAWAIIAN CHICKEN AND PINEAPPLE CURRY

- 2 cups coconut milk [1]
- ½ cup minced onion
- ⅓ cup butter
- ⅓ cup flour
- 4 teaspoons curry powder
- 1 teaspoon salt
- ½ teaspoon Ac'cent
- ½ teaspoon ginger
- 2 cups chicken broth
- 3 cups diced cooked chicken
- 1 cup cubed fresh pineapple

Prepare coconut milk as directed below, if not obtainable fresh. Cook onion in butter until soft but not brown. Blend in flour, curry powder, salt, Ac'cent and ginger. Add coconut milk and broth. Cook over low heat, stirring constantly, until thickened. Add chicken and pineapple. Heat thoroughly. Serve with fluffy rice and curry accompaniments, such as chutney, raisins, shredded coconut, macadamia nuts (or peanuts), etc. Makes 6 to 8 servings.

[1] *To make coconut milk:* Pour 2 cups hot milk over 4 cups grated fresh coconut or contents of 2 packages or cans of flaked coconut. Let stand 30 minutes. Strain through double cheesecloth, pressing to remove all liquid. Discard coconut. Chill coconut milk until ready to use. Makes 2 cups.

FLORIDA KEY LIME PIE

1 envelope (1 tablespoon) unflavored gelatine
¼ cup cold water
4 eggs, separated
1 cup sugar, divided
⅓ cup lime juice
½ teaspoon salt
2 teaspoons grated lime peel
Green food coloring

Soften gelatine in cold water. Beat egg yolks; add ½ cup sugar, lime juice and salt. Cook over hot water, stirring constantly until thickened. Add grated peel and gelatine; stir until gelatine is dissolved. Tint pale green with food coloring. Cool. Beat egg whites stiff but not dry; add remaining sugar slowly, beating after each addition; fold into lime mixture. Pour into baked 9-inch pieshell; chill until firm. Garnish top with halved white grapes and mint sprigs to resemble grape clusters.

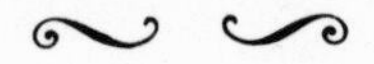

Menu

FORMAL DINNER

LEMON SOUP *

DUCKLING FLAMBÉ *

(WITH WILD RICE AND BUTTERED PECAN STUFFING)

ITALIAN GREEN BEANS CAULIFLOWER AU GRATIN

GARLIC BREAD

ENDIVE SALAD WITH ROQUEFORT DRESSING

CHOCOLATE REFRIGERATOR CAKE

DEMITASSE

LEMON SOUP

½ cup rice
6 cups clear beef broth
2 egg yolks
3 tablespoons lemon juice
Water Cress

Simmer rice in meat broth until rice is very soft, about 30 minutes. Beat 2 egg yolks; combine with lemon juice. Stir egg-lemon mixture into 1 cup hot broth. Remove remaining broth from heat. When broth stops bubbling, stir in egg mixture. Serve immediately, topped with Water Cress. Serves 6.

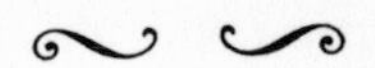

DUCKLING FLAMBÉ

2 Long Island ducklings
Salt
1 unpeeled orange
Ginger ale
4 cups cooked wild rice
¼ teaspoon cinnamon
1½ cups buttered sautéed pecans
1 cup apricot brandy
2 cups cooked diced apples
Sugar
1 cup cognac

Clean ducklings. Rub insides with salt. Insert ½ unpeeled orange in each cavity. Roast in very hot oven, 500°, for 10 minutes. Lower heat to 375° and roast until done (20 minutes per pound), basting often with ginger ale. Meanwhile combine wild rice, pecans, cinnamon, apricot brandy and apples. At the end of half the cooking time remove orange halves and stuff ducklings with wild rice mixture. Finish roasting. Place ducklings on hot platter; sprinkle with sugar and pour warm cognac over them. Ignite. Makes 8 servings.

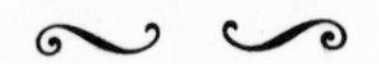

Menu

FORMAL LUNCHEON

CURRIED CRABMEAT SOUP *

CHEESE STRAWS

CHICKEN SALAD MOUSSE *

ASPARAGUS VINAIGRETTE

HOT ROLLS

CRÊPES MAGNOLIA *

TEA COFFEE

CURRIED CRABMEAT SOUP

4 cups milk
2 onion slices
3 stalks celery
2 sprigs parsley
2 cups light cream
½ cup melted butter
1 tablespoon curry powder, or to taste
½ cup flour
2 teaspoons salt
⅛ teaspoon pepper
2 cups flaked fresh crabmeat
¼ cup sauterne

Scald milk with onion, celery and parsley; strain. Add cream to scalded milk. Melt butter; blend in curry powder, flour, salt and pepper. Add milk mixture. Stir over low heat until smooth and thickened. Add crabmeat and sauterne. Heat through. Makes 8 servings.

CHICKEN SALAD MOUSSE

3 envelopes unflavored gelatine
½ cup cold water
6 egg yolks, slightly beaten
½ teaspoon paprika
Dash of cayenne
½ teaspoon Ac'cent
Salt to taste
2 cups chicken broth
2 cups cooked, finely-ground chicken
2 tablespoons minced parsley
1 tablespoon minced onion
1 tablespoon lemon juice
2 cups heavy cream, whipped

Soften gelatine in cold water. Combine egg yolks, paprika, cayenne, Ac'cent and salt in top of double boiler; gradually stir in chicken broth. Cook over hot water, stirring constantly, until mixture thickens. Add softened gelatine; stir until dissolved. Chill until consistency of unbeaten egg whites; stir in chicken, parsley, onion and lemon juice. Fold in whipped cream, blending gently but thoroughly. Taste; add additional salt, if needed. Turn into oiled 10½ x 5 x 2½-inch loaf pan; chill until firm. Unmold on salad greens. Garnish with radish roses and unpeeled, scored cucumber slices. Can also be made of leftover ham, turkey, crabmeat, shrimp or lobster. Makes 8 to 10 servings.

CRÊPES MAGNOLIA

1 cup sifted enriched flour
1 tablespoon sugar
Few grains salt
3 eggs
1 cup milk
2 tablespoons melted butter
1 teaspoon grated lemon peel
½ cup tart jelly or jam
1 pony brandy

Mix and sift flour, sugar and salt. Beat eggs; add to dry ingredients. Add milk; stir until smooth. Add melted butter. Strain through a fine sieve. Add lemon peel. Let stand two hours. Melt ½ teaspoon butter in 7-inch skillet. Pour in a thin layer of batter. When set and brown on underside, turn and brown on other side (about 1 minute each side). Repeat until batter is used (8 crêpes). Spread with jam; roll up. Put in very hot heat-proof serving dish; sprinkle with sugar. Pour warm brandy over all; ignite. Makes 8 servings.

Menu

BARBECUE AL FRESCO

CRISP RAW VEGETABLE RELISHES ON CHIPPED ICE

BARBECUED FILET OF BEEF *

CORN RELISH

ASPARAGUS PARMESAN

FOIL-ROASTED POTATOES WITH SOUR CREAM AND CHIVES

CHILLED WHOLE WATERMELON WITH CHAMPAGNE *

ICED BEVERAGES

BARBECUED FILET OF BEEF

Filet of beef (tenderloin) is thicker at one end than the other; thus, after broiling, you have rare, medium or well-done steak all at once. Let your guests have their choice. Have beef at room temperature. Put it on the barbecue spit and insert the spit forks. Arrange hot briquets at the rear of the spit; knock off the gray ash. Place a drip pan in front of briquets, under the spit. Attach the spit and start the motor. Basting during barbecuing is not necessary. As the spit turns, the fat bastes the meat and keeps it juicy. Allow about 45 minutes' barbecuing time. When done, remove the meat from the spit. Sprinkle with salt and coarse, freshly ground black pepper. Cut in crosswise slices and serve at once.

CHILLED WHOLE WATERMELON WITH CHAMPAGNE

Select a large, fully ripe watermelon. At one end cut out a deep plug 3 inches in diameter and cone-shaped. Stand watermelon on end. Fill cone-shaped cavity slowly with champagne. Replace plug; seal firmly with cellophane tape. Chill about 10 hours. To serve, cut off a lengthwise slice from the top of watermelon, deep enough to remove all rind. Scoop out servings with scoop or dipper-type spoon. Number of servings depends on size of melon—12 to 16.

Menu

INFORMAL LUNCHEON

EGG DROP SOUP

BUTTERFLY SHRIMP WITH HOT MUSTARD

CHINESE SALAD BOWL *

MIXED PRESERVED FRUITS

FORTUNE COOKIES

TEA

CHINESE SALAD BOWL
MAIN COURSE

- 1 package (1⅓ cups) pre-cooked rice
- 2 cups cooked green peas
- 1 can water chestnuts
- 1 can bean sprouts
- 1 head escarole
- ½ cup mayonnaise
- ½ cup dairy sour cream
- 1 teaspoon celery seed
- ½ teaspoon Ac'cent
- 1 cup roast pork cut in thin strips

Cook rice according to directions on package. Chill; place in salad bowl. Add peas. Drain water chestnuts; slice; add. Drain bean sprouts; add. Tear escarole leaves into small pieces; add. Combine mayonnaise, sour cream, celery seed and Ac'cent; beat well; pour into salad bowl. Toss until all ingredients are well-mixed. Scatter strips of pork on top. Makes 6 to 8 servings.

Menu

INFORMAL DINNER

JELLIED MADRILÈNE WITH CHIVES

CHICKEN VICTOR WITH DUMPLINGS *

ESCAROLE SALAD

SEVEN-LAYER CAKE

TEA COFFEE

CHICKEN VICTOR WITH DUMPLINGS

- 1 roasting chicken (3½ lbs.), disjointed
- 4 cups water
- 1 small onion, chopped
- 2 stalks celery, sliced
- 1 teaspoon salt
- ⅛ teaspoon pepper
- 1 cup sifted enriched flour
- 2 teaspoons baking powder
- ½ teaspoon sugar
- ½ teaspoon salt
- 2 tablespoons butter
- 1 egg, well beaten
- ⅓ cup milk
- ¼ pound snow peas, cooked
- 1 can water chestnuts, sliced
- 1 tablespoon lemon juice

Put chicken in kettle with water, onion, celery, salt and pepper. Bring to boil; simmer 45 minutes. Remove chicken; strain broth. Skin chicken; return to strained broth. Bring to boil. Meanwhile, mix and sift flour, baking powder, sugar and salt; cut in butter. Combine egg and milk; add to flour mixture; mix with a fork to soft dough. Drop by small spoonfuls into kettle, letting dough rest on pieces of chicken. Cook 10 minutes, uncovered; cover; cook 10 minutes longer. Remove dumplings and chicken to hot platter; keep warm. Add lemon juice to broth; thicken broth, if desired. Combine hot snow peas and sliced water chestnuts; add to platter. Pour some of the gravy over chicken. Serve remaining gravy separately.

Menu

FORMAL DINNER

BLINIS *

MEXICAN CHICKEN WITH FRUITS *

GREEN BEANS WITH SLICED BRAZIL NUTS

ROMAINE AND CHICORY SALAD

BREAD STICKS

HAZELNUT TORTE *

TEA COFFEE

BLINIS

1 cup sifted enriched flour
½ teaspoon salt
1 cup milk
2 eggs, slightly beaten
Caviar
Sour cream

Combine flour, salt and milk; beat smooth. Add eggs; mix well. Let stand 1 hour. Pour small amounts of batter to make cakes about 2½ inches in diameter on hot griddle. Brown on both sides; continue until all batter is used. Spread with caviar and roll up. Place, seam side down, close together on greased pie plates. Put in hot oven, 400°, for 5 minutes just before serving. Serve hot, topped with sour cream. Makes about 36 small blinis.

MEXICAN CHICKEN WITH FRUITS

2 frying chickens, disjointed
3 cups boiling water
2 tablespoons chili powder
¼ teaspoon pepper
½ teaspoon cinnamon
2 tablespoons grated onion
1½ teaspoons salt
2 cups orange juice
4 oranges, sectioned
1½ teaspoons sugar
2 avocados
½ pound grapes in season

Cover chicken with boiling water; add chili powder, pepper, cinnamon, grated onion and salt. Simmer 1 hour. Arrange chicken in baking pan. Add orange juice to broth in which chicken was cooked; heat; pour over chicken. Arrange orange sections on chicken; sprinkle with sugar. Bake in moderate oven, 375°, ½ hour. Remove chicken and fruits to serving platter; garnish with avocado slices and grapes. Serve gravy separately. Makes 6 to 8 servings.

HAZELNUT TORTE

2 cups shelled hazelnuts
½ cup sifted enriched flour
½ teaspoon instant coffee
½ teaspoon Dutch process cocoa
6 eggs, separated
1 cup sugar, divided
1 teaspoon grated lemon peel
1 teaspoon rum
½ teaspoon vanilla
Butter-cream frosting [1]

Grate hazelnuts. Set aside 1½ cups for frosting (there should be a little more than 4 cups left). Mix and sift flour, coffee, and cocoa; add to larger portion of hazelnuts; blend thoroughly. Divide mixture into 4 equal portions. Beat egg yolks; add ½ cup of the sugar gradually; beat until very thick and fluffy. Beat in lemon peel, rum and vanilla. Beat egg whites until frothy; add remaining sugar slowly while beating. Beat until soft peaks form. Gently spread egg yolk mixture over beaten egg whites. Spoon 1 portion hazelnut mixture over egg whites and gently fold until batter is *partially* blended. Repeat with second and third portions of hazelnut mixture. Spoon last portion over batter and gently fold until just blended. *Do not overmix.* Grease bottoms of two 9-inch round layer cake pans with removable bottoms. Gently spoon equal amount of batter into each, spreading to edges of pan. Bake at 350° 25 to 30 minutes or until top springs back when touched with fingertip. Cool; remove from pans. Cut one of the layers in half, crosswise. Fill and frost the three layers, placing uncut side of split layer next to plate. Chill. Makes 12 to 16 servings.

[1] *To make butter-cream frosting:*

6 egg yolks
¾ cup sugar
½ teaspoon cornstarch
¾ cup light cream
2 teaspoons vanilla
1½ cups sweet butter
1½ cups grated hazelnuts

Beat egg yolks until thick and lemon-colored. Combine sugar and cornstarch; add gradually to egg yolks, beating constantly. Add cream gradually, stirring until well blended. Cook over hot water, stirring constantly, until thickened (about 18 to 20 minutes). Remove from heat; stir in vanilla. Chill. Cream butter until fluffy. Add chilled mixture gradually to butter, beating after each addition until just blended. If frosting curdles, beat again until smooth. If necessary, chill until firm enough to spread. Blend in grated hazelnuts.

Menu

FORMAL DINNER

JELLIED CONSOMMÉ WITH PERNOD *

CELERY BLACK OLIVES RADISHES

FILET OF BEEF IN PASTRY CASE *

SUMMER SQUASH CIRCLES BROCCOLI IN BLACK BUTTER

CRESS AND ENDIVE SALAD WITH

DANISH BLUE CHEESE DRESSING

DINNER ROLLS

FRESH FREESTONE PEACH HALVES WITH MELBA SAUCE *

JELLIED CONSOMMÉ WITH PERNOD

Add 1 teaspoon Pernod for each cup of consommé before jelling.

FILET OF BEEF IN PASTRY CASE

2 cups sifted enriched flour
¾ teaspoon salt
⅓ cup shortening
⅓ cup butter
4 tablespoons ice water (approx.)
1 filet of beef (3½ to 4 pounds)
4 tablespoons pâté de foie gras

Mix and sift flour and salt. Cut in shortening and butter until flour-fat particles are about the size of small peas. Sprinkle 1 tablespoon of the ice water over mixture; mix in lightly with a fork. Continue adding ice water in this way until pastry gathers around fork in a soft ball. Roll out thin in rectangular shape on lightly floured board. Spread top of filet of beef with pâté de foie gras. Place, pâté side *down,* in center of pastry. Bring sides of pastry up over filet; trim off any excess and seal seam with cold water. Trim pastry off ends. Place seam side down in jelly roll pan, 15 x 10 x 1-inch. Cut slits at 1-inch intervals in pastry, as a guide to slicing. Bake at 450° for 20 minutes. Reduce heat to 350°; bake 18 to 20 minutes longer, or until pastry is golden brown and meat rare (a meat thermometer, inserted through pastry and half way into thickest part of filet, is a sure guide to degree of rareness desired). Makes 8 to 12 servings.

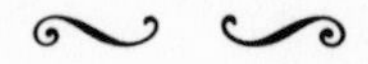

MELBA SAUCE

½ cup sugar
2 cups fresh raspberries
½ cup currant jelly
1½ teaspoons cornstarch
1 tablespoon cold water

Add sugar to raspberries in a saucepan; mash. Add jelly; bring to boil. Mix cornstarch and water; add. Cook, stirring, until clear. Strain through fine sieve. Cool. Makes 6 servings.

Menu

INFORMAL DINNER

ONION SOUP

VICTOR'S LAMB CHOPS *

SWEET-SOUR BEETS SCALLOPED POTATOES

TOSSED GREEN SALAD WITH ITALIAN DRESSING

APPLE CHARLOTTE *

TEA COFFEE

VICTOR'S LAMB CHOPS

6 loin lamb chops
1 garlic clove
Salt and pepper to taste

Select thick loin lamb chops; broil quickly on both sides until browned, about 10 minutes. Transfer to oven. Add 1 slashed garlic clove to drippings with salt and pepper to taste. Bake at 350° for 20 to 30 minutes, depending on how well-done desired. Makes 6 servings.

APPLE CHARLOTTE

Kuchen Dough

1 cup sifted enriched flour
½ teaspoon baking powder
¼ teaspoon salt
2 tablespoons sugar
2½ tablespoons butter
2 eggs beaten
2 tablespoons milk

Filling

5 cups sliced raw apples
½ cup golden seedless raisins
⅔ cup sugar
1 teaspoon cinnamon
1 tablespoon grated lemon peel

Topping

1 cup whipping cream
½ teaspoon almond extract

To make dough: Mix and sift flour, baking powder, salt and sugar. Work butter in smoothly with wooden spoon. Beat in eggs. Stir in milk. Grease 8-inch spring form pan. With rubber spatula or spoon, spread dough on bottom and partway up sides of spring form pan (top edge will be ragged).

To make filling: Cook apple slices and raisins in enough water to cover until apples are just tender, but have not lost their shape; drain. Combine sugar, cinnamon and lemon peel; stir gently into apples and raisins. Spoon into dough-lined spring form pan. Bake at 425° for 50 to 60 minutes or until crust is deep golden brown and filling is firm. Serve hot, topped with almond-flavored whipped cream.

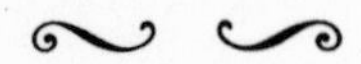

Menu

FORMAL LUNCHEON

ARTICHOKES VINAIGRETTE

CRABMEAT SOUFFLÉ *

GRILLED TOMATOES

COLE SLAW WITH CARAWAY SEED

CANDLELIGHT CHEESE CAKE

TEA COFFEE

CRABMEAT SOUFFLÉ

4 tablespoons butter
1 tablespoon minced onion
1 tablespoon minced green pepper
1 tablespoon minced celery
3 tablespoons flour
½ teaspoon salt
⅛ teaspoon pepper
1 cup milk
4 eggs, separated
2 cups cooked flaked crabmeat

Melt butter; add onion, green pepper and celery; cook until soft but not brown. Blend in flour, salt and pepper. Add milk; cook, stirring until thickened. Beat egg yolks until thick and lemon colored; stir slowly into white sauce. Add crabmeat. Beat egg whites stiff; fold in. Turn into buttered 1 quart soufflé dish or casserole; set dish in pan of hot water; bake at 350° about 50 minutes or until soufflé looks dry on top. Serve at once. Makes 6 servings.

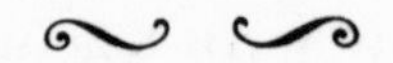

Menu

GARDEN PARTY LUNCHEON

COCKTAILS

TRAY OF SMOKED SALMON, SMOKED STURGEON AND

CAVIAR WITH THIN BUTTERED PUMPERNICKEL

JELLIED HAM AND CHICKEN LOAF *

VICTOR'S ALL-WHITE SALAD PLATTER *

ROLLED CRESS SANDWICHES

PINEAPPLE SHERBET WITH GREEN CRÈME DE MENTHE

TEA COFFEE

JELLIED HAM AND CHICKEN LOAF

4 cups chicken broth
2 envelopes unflavored gelatine
½ cup Rhine wine
2 cups ground cooked ham
4 or 5 hard-cooked eggs, shelled
2 cups ground, well-seasoned cooked chicken

Bring chicken broth to boiling point. Soften gelatine in wine; dissolve in hot broth. Pour gelatine mixture in bottom of 9 x 5 x 3-inch loaf pan to a depth of ½-inch. Chill until almost set. Spread ham on top. Place whole hard-cooked eggs in a lengthwise row down center of ham layer. Cover with ground chicken. Pour remaining gelatine mixture slowly into pan. Chill until set. Unmold on platter. Garnish with cress, stuffed olives and pickle fans. Makes 8 to 10 servings.

VICTOR'S ALL-WHITE SALAD PLATTER

On a large platter or silver tray arrange grapefruit sections, spears of canned white Belgian asparagus, water chestnuts, cauliflower, fresh pineapple chunks, apple slices, hearts of palm, artichoke bottoms, cold braised hearts of celery, and white radishes. Sprinkle curls of fresh coconut over all. Serve with tart French dressing.

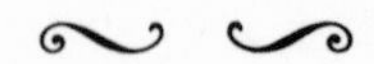

Menu

INFORMAL DINNER

HOT TOMATO JUICE

ROAST LEG OF LAMB *

CANDIED YAMS

ASPARAGUS WITH DRAWN BUTTER

ENDIVE VINAIGRETTE

VICTOR'S LEMON MERINGUE PIE *

TEA COFFEE

ROAST LEG OF LAMB

1 leg of lamb (about 6 lbs.)
1 garlic clove, sliced
1 tablespoon cut chives
1 to 1½ teaspoons salt
¼ teaspoon coarsely ground black pepper
1 tablespoon paprika
2 cups dairy sour cream
1 cup hot water
2 tablespoons flour
½ cup cold water
Salt and black pepper to taste

Make small gashes in surface of meat; tuck garlic slices down into gashes. Rub entire outside with chives, salt, pepper and paprika. Place meat on platter. Coat completely with sour cream. Chill, uncovered, in refrigerator about 4 to 6 hours or until sour cream has formed a dry crust. Place meat, cream side up, on rack in shallow pan. Roast uncovered in a slow oven, 325°, about 2 hours. Remove roast from oven; crack surface with knife, so that crust falls into pan, forming basis of gravy. Return to oven; continue baking about ½ to 1 hour longer or until done.[1] Lift roast to serving platter; keep warm. *For gravy, pour hot water into roasting pan; place over moderate heat; stir flour and water together until smooth; gradually add to boiling liquid in roasting pan, stirring constantly until thickened and smooth; add salt and pepper to taste.* Makes 8 to 12 servings.

OUR VICTOR'S LEMON MERINGUE PIE

7 tablespoons cornstarch
1½ cups sugar
¼ teaspoon salt
1½ cups hot water
3 egg yolks, beaten
½ cup lemon juice
1 teaspoon grated lemon peel
2 tablespoons butter
1 cup whipping cream
1 10-inch baked pie shell

---

[1] Allow 30 minutes per pound for medium done; 35 to 38 minutes per pound for well done.

Mix cornstarch, sugar and salt in saucepan. Stir in hot water gradually; bring to boil over direct heat; then cook for 5 to 7 minutes over medium heat, stirring constantly until thick and clear. Remove from heat. Stir several spoonfuls of this hot mixture into beaten egg yolks; mix well. Pour egg yolk mixture back into saucepan. Bring to boil; then cook over low heat for 3 to 4 minutes, stirring constantly. Remove from heat; gradually add lemon juice, lemon peel and butter; cool. Whip cream; fold in; pour into cooled baked pie shell. Top with meringue.[1]

[1] *To make meringue:*

3 eggs whites (at room temperature)
1 teaspoon lemon juice
6 tablespoons sugar
Anise Seed

Place egg whites in deep, medium-size bowl; add lemon juice. Beat until whites stand in soft peaks before adding sugar. Add sugar gradually, beat well after each addition; continue beating until all sugar is used and whites stand in firm, glossy peaks. Spread meringue over cool filling—start at edges and work toward center of pie; be sure to attach meringue securely to edges of crust. Scatter anise seed over meringue. Bake at 350° for 15 to 20 minutes, or until golden brown. Cool before serving.

Menu

INFORMAL DINNER

NUMAKI *

SPARERIBS KINSALE *

SWEET-SOUR RED CABBAGE

FRENCH FRIED SWEET POTATOES

HEARTS OF LETTUCE WITH GARLIC FRENCH DRESSING

CHEESE AND FRUIT TRAY

TEA COFFEE

NUMAKI

Cooked chicken livers
Canned water chestnuts
Bacon slices

Cut cooked chicken livers into bite-size pieces. Slice canned water chestnuts. Wrap one piece of chicken liver and one slice of water chestnut in half a strip bacon; secure with wooden picks. Broil slowly until bacon is crisp. Serve hot.

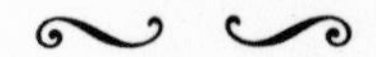

SPARERIBS KINSALE

1 rack spareribs (2 to 2½ pounds)
1 cup vinegar
2 tablespoons brown sugar
1 tablespoon salt
¼ teaspoon coarsely ground black pepper
½ garlic clove, bruised

Have spareribs cut in serving-size pieces at market. Remove excess fat. Combine remaining ingredients; pour over spareribs. Let stand 2 hours, turning occasionally. Remove spareribs to shallow roasting pan (save vinegar marinade). Cover pan with foil. Roast at 325° for ½ hour. Pour off fat. Roast ½ hour longer. Again pour off fat. Pour vinegar marinade over ribs. Increase heat to 400°. Roast, uncovered, for 45 minutes, basting often with marinade in pan. Makes 6 servings.

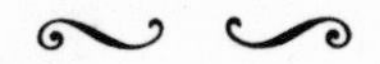

Menu

MIDNIGHT SUPPER

TONGUE IN ASPIC   CHICKEN HASH IN RAMEKINS

MYSTERY MACARONI SALAD *

FINGER BREAD AND BUTTER SANDWICHES

WATERMELON RIND PICKLES

LEMON SHERBET   CHOCOLATE WAFERS

COFFEE

MYSTERY MACARONI SALAD

1 tablespoon salt
3 quarts boiling water
2 cups elbow macaroni (8 oz.)
2 medium-sized apples, diced
¼ cup vinegar
1 8-oz. jar herring fillets in cream, diced
⅓ cup sliced sweet gherkins
1 large sweet onion, sliced thin
1 teaspoon salt
½ cup dairy sour cream
½ cup mayonnaise
1 tablespoon chopped dill
Crisp salad greens

Add 1 tablespoon salt to rapidly boiling water. Gradually add macaroni so that water continues to boil. Cook uncovered, stirring occasionally, until tender. Drain in colander. Rinse with cold water; drain and chill. Meanwhile, combine apples, vinegar, herring, gherkins, onion, 1 teaspoon salt, sour cream, mayonnaise, and dill; mix well and chill. Combine apple mixture and macaroni; toss lightly but thoroughly. Serve on salad greens. Makes 6 to 8 servings.

Section Two

SKY HIGH

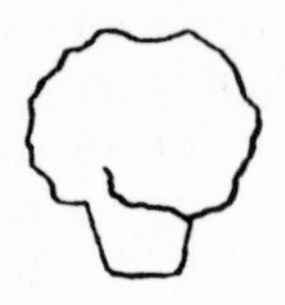

FROM SKY HIGH, my Fifth Avenue penthouse, there is a panoramic view of Central Park, a glimpse of the Hudson, a commanding view of the East River and a variety of metropolitan skylines unmatched in the world. And my menus here are, on the whole, suited to cosmopolitan palates. I must mention that I always try to make the final meal—both at Kinsale and Sky High—the most dramatic of all, something like a third-act climax.

The fare is varied in my city home. I never forget the favorite dishes of my friends and what I served when they were here last, so that few people can complain of "having the same old thing" at Sky High. One of the favorite menus of urban guests is quite simple but takes careful doing—rare roast beef and Yorkshire pudding, preceded by a clear broth subtly flavored with leeks. The Quiche Lorraine is extremely popular in New York and so is the boned duckling in aspic, garnished with glazed oranges and Bing cherries.

Beef Burgundy, which Rosie always referred to facetiously as pot roast, is another dish fancied by city dwellers. As for desserts especially exciting in an urban atmosphere, try the Coffee Pearadise and Apple Pie.

Menu

FORMAL LUNCHEON

FRESH CANTALOUPE, HONEY DEW AND WATERMELON BALLS

(IN AMERICAN WHITE WINE)

CHICKEN AND SWEETBREADS VOL AU VENT *

GREEN PEAS WITH COCKTAIL ONIONS

TINY HOT BISCUITS

TOSSED SALAD WITH HERB GARDEN DRESSING *

COFFEE PEARADISE *

CHICKEN AND SWEETBREADS VOL AU VENT

1 pound veal sweetbreads
2 cups cubed cooked chicken
3 tablespoons butter
3 tablespoons flour
1 teaspoon paprika
Dash white pepper
¾ teaspoon salt
2 cups chicken broth
1 cup light cream
3 tablespoons Amontillado sherry

Precook sweetbreads: drop into boiling water; add 1 teaspoon salt; simmer 25 minutes; drain; hold under cold, running water and slip off membrane with fingers. With a sharp knife remove dark veins and thick connective tissue. Break into pieces; combine with chicken. Melt butter; blend in flour, paprika, pepper and salt. Combine broth and cream; add all at once. Cook and stir over low heat until smooth and thickened. Add chicken and sweetbreads, and sherry. Heat through. Serve in hot patty shells. Makes 8 servings.

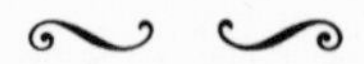

HERB GARDEN SALAD DRESSING

1½ tablespoons sugar
1 teaspoon salt
¼ teaspoon Ac'cent
2 teaspoons prepared mustard
¼ teaspoon dried rosemary
⅛ teaspoon dried thyme
¼ teaspoon dried savory
2 tablespoons flour
1 egg, slightly beaten
¾ cup milk
¼ cup lemon juice
1 tablespoon butter
½ cup light cream

In top of double boiler combine sugar, salt, Ac'cent, mustard, herbs and flour. Add egg; blend well. Add milk slowly, blending well. Add lemon juice. Cook over hot water, stirring constantly, until thickened. Add butter; stir until melted. Add cream. Cool, then chill. Makes about 1½ cups dressing.

COFFEE PEARADISE

1 tablespoon unflavored gelatine
2 tablespoons cold coffee
6 tablespoons sugar
1 cup hot strong coffee
½ cup pear syrup
5 to 6 canned pear halves
1 cup heavy cream, whipped
½ teaspoon vanilla

Soften gelatine in cold coffee; add sugar. Pour hot coffee over all and stir until dissolved. Add pear syrup. Arrange pear halves in bottom of 10-inch ring mold. Add part of gelatine mixture to a depth of about ½ inch; chill. Chill remaining gelatine mixture until slightly thickened. Whip cream and vanilla together; fold into remaining gelatine mixture. Spoon into ring mold; chill until firm. Unmold on serving platter. Serve with additional whipped cream if desired.

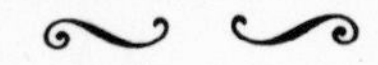

Menu

BUFFET

COCKTAILS

DIAMOND CHICKEN LIVER PÂTÉ *

ASSORTED CRISP CRACKERS

BONED DUCKLING IN ASPIC

(GARNISHED WITH GLAZED ORANGES AND BLACK

PITTED BING CHERRIES)

CREAMED CHIPPED BEEF ON POLENTA SQUARES

TINY WHOLE WHEAT ROLLS

COFFEE-RUM CREAM CAKE *

DIAMOND LIVER PÂTÉ

- 1 small onion, minced
- 1 pound butter, divided
- 1 pound fresh chicken livers, diced
- 1½ cups clear chicken broth, divided
- 4 tablespoons Marsala wine
- ½ teaspoon paprika
- ⅛ teaspoon allspice
- ½ teaspoon salt
- ⅛ teaspoon white pepper or Tabasco
- 1 clove garlic, minced
- ⅓ cup cognac
- 1 cup roasted walnuts, chopped
- 1 envelope unflavored gelatine

Sauté onion in ½ pound butter until tender. Add diced chicken livers; cook for 10 minutes, stirring occasionally. Add half the chicken broth, Marsala wine, paprika, allspice, salt, pepper and garlic. Cook five minutes more. Place mixture in electric blender. Gradually add remaining butter (melted) and cognac. Blend until smooth. Stir in walnuts. In saucepan, sprinkle gelatine over rest of broth. Heat; stir until gelatine is dissolved. Pour part of gelatine broth into 6-cup mold. Chill for 10 minutes. Fill mold with chicken liver mixture; top with remaining broth. Keep in refrigerator for at least 6 hours before unmolding and serving.

COFFEE-RUM CREAM CAKE

Cake Batter

- 2 eggs
- ¼ teaspoon salt
- 1 cup sugar
- 1 teaspoon rum flavoring
- ½ cup milk
- 1 tablespoon butter
- 1 cup sifted enriched flour
- 1 teaspoon baking powder

Beat eggs until thick and light. Beat in salt, sugar, and flavoring. Heat milk and butter to boiling point; beat in. Mix and sift flour and baking powder; beat in. Turn into greased and floured layer cake pan 9 inches in diameter and 1½ inches deep. Bake in moderate oven, 350°, for 35 to 40 minutes. Remove from pan. Spoon coffee-rum syrup slowly over warm cake, covering entire surface until syrup is all absorbed. Let stand until cold. Split carefully into 2 layers; fill with rum-cream filling. Garnish top with Damson plum preserves and whipped cream put through ribbon tip of pastry tube.

Coffee-Rum Syrup

Combine 1 cup sugar and 1 cup strong coffee; stir over low heat until sugar dissolves. Boil 3 minutes; cool. Add ¼ cup rum.

Rum Cream Filling

⅓ cup sugar
¼ cup flour
⅛ teaspoon salt
1 cup milk
2 egg yolks or 1 whole slightly beaten egg
1 tablespoon rum

Combine sugar, flour and salt in top of double boiler; add milk; stir over low heat until thickened. Cook, covered, over hot water for 10 minutes. Add a little of the hot mixture to egg yolks; combine with remaining hot mixture; cook 2 minutes longer, stirring constantly. Chill. Add rum.

Menu

FORMAL DINNER

ARTICHOKES SKY HIGH *

CLEAR TURTLE BROTH

BEEF BURGUNDY *

WILD RICE WITH PISTACHIO NUTS

BEET AND ONION RING SALAD

COINTREAU CHIFFON PIE *

DEMITASSE

ARTICHOKES SKY HIGH

12 cooked, chilled artichoke bottoms
12 cold poached eggs
Thin mustard mayonnaise
6 truffles

For each serving, mask artichoke heart and poached egg with mustard mayonnaise. Garnish with ½ truffle.

Note: The eggs should be poached in water in which anchovy paste has been dissolved. (Use about 2 teaspoons anchovy paste to a pint of water.)

BEEF BURGUNDY

⅓ cup butter
4 pounds boned sirloin steak, cubed
2 garlic cloves
4 medium onions, sliced
1½ cups water
3 cups Burgundy wine, divided
1 tablespoon salt
¾ teaspoon Ac'cent
½ teaspoon pepper
¾ teaspoon savory
½ teaspoon oregano
⅓ cup enriched flour
Dairy sour cream

Melt butter; add beef; brown on all sides. Add garlic, onions, water, 1½ cups Burgundy, salt, Ac'cent and pepper. Cover; simmer gently for 1 hour, or until meat is tender. Remove garlic. Add remaining Burgundy, savory, and oregano. Simmer 15 minutes longer. Thicken with flour mixed smooth with ½ cup water. Simmer, stirring, until smooth. Top with spoonfuls of sour cream. Makes 12 servings.

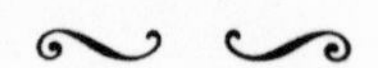

COINTREAU CHIFFON PIE

1 envelope unflavored gelatine
¼ cup cold water
4 eggs, separated
¾ cup sugar, divided
⅓ cup orange juice
¼ teaspoon salt
2 tablespoons Cointreau
1 tablespoon grated orange peel
1 9-inch baked pie shell

Soften gelatine in cold water. Beat egg yolks until thick and lemon-colored; beat in ½ cup sugar, orange juice, and salt. Cook over boiling water, stirring constantly, until thickened. Add softened gelatine; stir until gelatine dissolves. Add Cointreau and orange peel. Cool until mixture begins to stiffen. Beat egg whites; add remaining sugar gradually; beat until stiff and glossy; fold into gelatine mixture. Spoon into baked pie shell. Chill until firm. Garnish top with border of whipped cream. Sprinkle border with mixture of 1 tablespoon grated orange peel and 2 tablespoons finely chopped toasted almonds.

Menu

DINNER EN FAMILLE

BEEF BROTH WITH DUMPLINGS *

ROAST BEEF

FRESH GRATED HORSERADISH **YORKSHIRE PUDDING ***

ASPARAGUS WITH BUTTER SAUCE **BRAISED ONIONS**

HEARTS OF LETTUCE WITH DRESSING

APPLE PIE

COFFEE

BEEF BROTH WITH DUMPLINGS

1 cup finely chopped leeks (5 or 6 bulbs)
4 tablespoons butter, divided
2 quarts well-seasoned beef broth
¾ cup milk
½ teaspoon salt
6 tablespoons Cream of Rice
1 egg, slightly beaten
1 tablespoon minced parsley

Brown leeks well in 2 tablespoons butter; add to beef broth; heat to boiling. Meanwhile heat milk until small bubbles form. Sprinkle in salt and Cream of Rice, stirring constantly. Cook and stir until thickened, about 2 minutes. Add remaining 2 tablespoons butter; mix well. Stir in egg and parsley; blend until smooth; drop by half-teaspoons into boiling broth. Cover tightly. Cook about 10 minutes. Serve at once. Makes 12 servings.

YORKSHIRE PUDDING

2 eggs
1 egg yolk
1 cup milk
1 cup sifted enriched flour
½ teaspoon salt

Have all ingredients at room temperature. Beat eggs and egg yolk. Add about half the cup of milk. Add flour and salt; beat smooth. Add remaining milk; mix well. *Let stand* 1 hour. Beat again. Remove roast beef from oven; keep warm. Increase oven temperature to 450°. Pour enough fat from roasting pan into 10-inch square pan to cover bottom. Put pan in oven until hot. Pour batter into pan. When pudding has puffed and is beginning to brown (10 to 12 minutes) lower heat to 400°; after 10 minutes lower heat to 350°. Bake 15 minutes longer. Cut pudding into squares and serve around roast. Makes 6 to 8 servings.

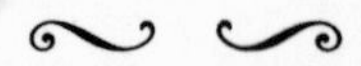

APPLE PIE

Pastry

1 tablespoon shortening
½ pound (2 sticks) butter
3 cups sifted enriched flour
½ cup ice water (approx.)

Filling

8 medium McIntosh apples
1 tablespoon lemon juice
¾ cup firmly packed brown sugar
¼ teaspoon nutmeg
½ teaspoon cinnamon
⅛ teaspoon cloves
1 tablespoon sugar
2 tablespoons water

Cut shortening and butter into flour with 2 knives until particles are the size of barley grains. Add ice water slowly, mixing with a fork, until dough gathers around fork in a ball. Divide dough in half. Roll out each half between sheets of waxed paper to make a circle about 12 inches in diameter. Fit one circle into 10-inch pie pan. Trim off edge. Slice apples; place in shallow baking dish. Sprinkle with lemon juice. Combine brown sugar and spices; scatter over apples. Bake in hot oven, 425°, until apples are soft and top lightly browned, about 20 minutes. During last 10 minutes of baking time, bake bottom crust of pie. Pour hot apples into pie pan. Adjust unbaked pastry circle on top; trim; press edges together and cut slits in center. Brush top with mixture of sugar and water. Continue baking until top crust is golden brown, about 25 minutes longer.

Menu

BUFFET

CHILLED VICHYSOISSE

BONED AND ROLLED ROAST TURKEY

KIDNEYS MADEIRA *

HOT POTATO SALAD *

CRANBERRY RELISH *

FRENCH VANILLA ICE CREAM

VIENNESE CHOCOLATE CHERRY TORTE *

TEA COFFEE

LAMB KIDNEYS IN MADEIRA SAUCE

18 lamb kidneys
½ pound mushrooms
1 small onion
5 tablespoons butter, divided
3 tablespoons flour
⅓ cup Madeira
½ cup consommé
1 tablespoon lemon juice
3 tablespoons chopped parsley
Salt and pepper
8 white bread rounds, ½-inch thick
Parsley and lemon wedges

Split kidneys; remove skin and fat. Slice mushroom stems; leave caps whole. Slice onion very thin; separate slices into rings. Brown kidneys quickly in 4 tablespoons butter. Reduce heat; remove kidneys. Add mushrooms and onions; cook 3 minutes, stirring frequently. Sprinkle with flour; stir gently until it disappears. Add wine and consommé. Cover; simmer 10 minutes. Add kidneys; simmer uncovered 10 minutes more. Remove from heat; add lemon juice, remaining butter, and parsley. Season to taste with salt and pepper. Cut large rounds of bread with a cookie cutter. Sauté bread rounds in additional butter until golden brown on both sides. To serve, place bread rounds on individual plates. Top with kidneys; garnish with parsley and lemon wedges. Serve very hot. Makes 6 servings.

HOT POTATO SALAD

2 medium onions
6 cups cubed, hot cooked potatoes
1 tablespoon minced parsley
⅔ cup vinegar
⅓ cup hot water
1 teaspoon sugar
1 egg
⅓ cup salad oil
Salt and pepper

Mince onions; add to potatoes with parsley. Heat vinegar and water; add sugar; stir until sugar dissolves. Beat egg slightly; add hot vinegar mixture and salad oil. Beat vigorously; pour over potato mixture. Stir with fork until well mixed. Season to taste. Heat. Makes 6 servings.

CRANBERRY RELISH

1⅔ cups sugar
1 cup water
4 cups fresh cranberries
1 cup seedless raisins
1½ teaspoons ginger
¼ teaspoon ground cloves
1 cinnamon stick, 2 inches long
1 onion, thinly sliced
1 apple, chopped
½ cup thinly sliced celery

Combine sugar, water, cranberries, raisins, and spices in saucepan. Cook until berries pop and mixture starts to thicken, about 20 minutes. Add remaining ingredients; simmer 15 to 20 minutes longer, or until relish is as thick as desired. Discard cinnamon stick. Ladle into hot sterilized jelly glasses; seal at once with paraffin. Makes about five 8-ounce glasses.

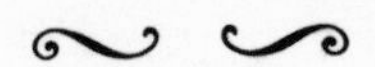

VIENNESE CHOCOLATE CHERRY TORTE

1½ cups butter
6 squares (6 oz.) unsweetened chocolate
3 cups sugar
6 eggs, beaten
3 cups sifted cake flour
¾ teaspoon baking powder
¾ teaspoon salt
1 No. 303 can (1 pound) pitted sour red cherries
1 tablespoon vanilla

Melt butter and chocolate together over hot water. Add sugar to beaten eggs gradually, while beating. Add chocolate mixture to egg mixture; beat hard for 1 minute. Mix and sift flour, baking powder, and salt. Drain cherries thoroughly; add to flour mixture; stir into chocolate-egg mixture. Stir in vanilla. Divide batter evenly among three greased and floured 10-inch layer-cake pans. Bake at 350° for 30 to 35 minutes. When cool, put together with sweetened whipped cream. Garnish top with whipped cream. Chill.

Menu

MIDNIGHT SUPPER

QUICHE LORRAINE *

CREAMED OYSTERS, MUSHROOMS, AND SHRIMP

MINTED PETITS POIS

TOSSED GREEN SALAD WITH CROUTONS

LEMON ICE CREAM

RASPBERRY PASTRIES *

DEMITASSE

QUICHE LORRAINE

½ cup grated Swiss cheese
¼ cup grated Parmesan cheese
¼ cup grated sharp cheddar cheese
9-inch unbaked pie shell
4 strips bacon, cooked crisp, and crumbled
4 eggs, slightly beaten
1 cup milk
1 cup heavy cream
Few grains nutmeg
½ teaspoon salt
¼ teaspoon pepper

Sprinkle grated cheese in pie shell; add crumbled bacon. Combine eggs, milk, cream, nutmeg, salt and pepper; mix well; pour into pie shell. Bake at 400° for about 40 minutes or until custard is well set.

RASPBERRY PASTRIES

1 cup butter
½ pound (8 oz. package) cream cheese
2 cups sifted enriched flour
1 teaspoon salt
Black raspberry jam

Combine butter and cream cheese and blend until smooth. Combine flour and salt; blend into butter mixture. Chill about ½ hour. Roll out about ¼ inch thick. Cut into 2½ inch squares. Spread each square with 1 teaspoon raspberry jam to within ¼ inch of edges. Roll up firmly. Place rolled edge down on ungreased baking sheet. Bake at 425° for about 12 minutes or until golden brown. Makes about 2½ dozen.*

* Can make more as it freezes very well and is so useful and wonderful as a main course for luncheon or a hearty cocktail accompaniment.

Menu

BUFFET LUNCHEON

COCKTAILS

AVOCADO SHRIMP DIP *

OYSTER LOAF *

MUSTARD RELISH MOLDS * SPINACH SOUFFLÉ *

HOT BUTTERFLAKE ROLLS

IRISH TRIFLE *

TEA COFFEE

AVOCADO SHRIMP DIP

2 ripe avocados
1 cup dairy sour cream
½ teaspoon Ac'cent
½ teaspoon salt
2 tablespoons prepared horseradish
1 small onion, grated

Mash avocados to smooth pulp with wooden spoon or electric blender. Whip in remaining ingredients. Makes about 2 cups. Serve with chilled, cooked shrimp.

OYSTER LOAF

1 (1 lb.) loaf unsliced white bread
1 cup butter, melted (approx.)
1 quart shucked raw oysters
2 eggs, beaten
¼ cup milk
½ teaspoon celery salt
½ teaspoon onion salt
¼ teaspoon pepper
Fine cracker crumbs
Fat or oil for shallow frying
½ pound bacon, cooked crisp

Trim crusts from top and sides of bread. Slice off loaf top 1 inch thick; set aside. Hollow out remaining loaf, leaving ⅜-inch-thick side walls and base, thus making a bread case. (Save left-over crumbs to use later in other dishes.) Brush cut-off top slice and inside and outside of bread loaf case with butter. Place both in baking pan; bake at 375° for 12 to 15 minutes or until pale golden; remove from oven. Drain oysters. Mix together eggs, milk, celery salt, onion salt and pepper; pour into shallow bowl. Dip oysters into cracker crumbs, then into egg mixture, and back into cracker crumbs until evenly coated. Fry oysters, without crowding, in 2-inch deep hot fat for about 2 minutes or until delicately browned; remove; drain on absorbent paper.

Place half of bacon in prepared bread case; set on heat-proof serving platter; fill with oysters; top with remaining bacon; cover with top slice; surround loaf with any remaining oysters. Bake in moderate oven, 375°, for 5 to 6 minutes or until piping hot. Makes 6 servings.

MUSTARD RELISH MOLDS

- 2 envelopes unflavored gelatine
- ½ cup cold water
- 1½ cups sugar
- 1½ tablespoons dry mustard
- 1½ teaspoons salt
- 2 teaspoons Ac'cent
- 2 cups cider vinegar
- 6 eggs, slightly beaten
- 1 cup finely diced celery
- 1 cup cooked green peas
- ½ cup diced green pepper
- 1 cup grated raw carrots

Soften gelatine in cold water. Combine in a saucepan sugar, mustard, salt, Ac'cent, vinegar, and eggs. Stir over low heat until thickened (do not boil). Add gelatine; stir until dissolved. Chill to consistency of unbeaten egg whites; fold in vegetables. Turn into 16 individual molds. Chill until set.

SPINACH SOUFFLÉ

- 4 tablespoons butter
- 1 tablespoon minced onion
- 1 tablespoon minced green pepper
- 1 tablespoon minced celery
- 3 tablespoons flour
- ½ teaspoon salt
- ⅛ teaspoon pepper
- 1 cup milk
- 4 eggs, separated
- 2 cups chopped cooked spinch, drained dry

Melt butter; add onion, green pepper, and celery; cook until soft but not brown. Blend in flour, salt and pepper. Add milk;

cook, stirring until thickened. Beat egg yolks until thick and lemon colored; stir slowly into white sauce. Add spinach. Beat egg whites stiff; fold in. Turn into buttered 1-quart soufflé dish or casserole; set dish in pan of hot water; bake at 350° for about 50 minutes or until soufflé looks dry on top. Serve at once. Makes 6 servings.

IRISH TRIFLE

2 dozen packaged lady-fingers
½ cup raspberry jam (approx.)
½ cup sweet sherry, divided
2 cups chilled soft custard[1]
6 almond macaroons, crumbled
1 cup whipping cream
1 tablespoon sugar
¼ cup slivered, toasted almonds

Split lady-fingers; put together again sandwich fashion with jam. Arrange 12 filled lady-fingers in a row in bottom of glass serving dish. Sprinkle with ¼ cup of the sherry. Arrange remaining lady-fingers on top, with row running in opposite direction; sprinkle with remaining wine. Pour custard over lady-fingers; chill. Top with crumbled macaroons. Whip cream, adding sugar gradually. Spread cream over macaroons. Scatter almonds over cream. Garnish with cherries glacé and angelica (can be purchased in small jars). Makes 8 servings.

[1] *Soft Custard*

2 cups milk
3 eggs or 6 egg yolks
¼ cup sugar
¼ teaspoon salt
1 teaspoon vanilla

Heat milk over hot water in double boiler until tiny bubbles appear around edge. Beat eggs or egg yolks slightly with a fork;

stir in sugar and salt. Add hot milk *slowly,* stirring constantly. Return mixture to double boiler; cook over hot (not boiling) water, stirring constantly until mixture coats spoon with thin film. Pour at once into cool bowl. Cool. Add vanilla. Cover; chill. Makes about 2 cups.

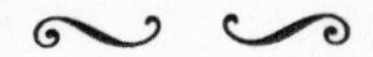

Menu

INFORMAL LUNCHEON

PROSCIUTTO HAM AND CRANSHAW MELON

TURKEY-FILLED CRÊPES *

GREEN BEANS COOKED IN CHICKEN CONSOMMÉ

TOMATO ASPIC SALAD

CHOCOLATE MOUSSE

TEA COFFEE

TURKEY-FILLED CRÊPES

Batter

4 eggs, beaten
1 cup milk, divided
1 cup sifted, enriched flour
1 cup melted butter
½ teaspoon salt

Filling

3 tablespoons butter
1 tablespoon minced onion
4 tablespoons flour
1 cup milk
1½ cups finely diced turkey
¼ cup minced black olives
1 tablespoon finely diced pimiento
1 teaspoon salt
Few grains pepper
¼ teaspoon paprika

To make batter: Combine eggs and ½ cup milk; add slowly to flour; add remaining ½ cup milk; beat smooth. Strain. Add cooled, melted butter and salt. Bake on ungreased hot griddle (very thin). Roll up while warm. Makes 12 crêpes, about 6 inches in diameter.

To make filling: Melt butter; add onion; cook until soft but not brown. Blend in flour; add milk; stir over low heat until thick. Add remaining ingredients. Unroll crêpes; spread with filling; re-roll. Place, seam side down, on baking sheet. Reheat at 350°. Serve with turkey giblet gravy or mushroom gravy. Makes 6 servings.

Menu

LUNCHEON FOR LES GIRLS

CRESS, MUSHROOM, AND LOBSTER BISQUE *

PÂTÉ BISCUITS *

FRUIT SALAD MANDARIN *

SHERRY DESSERT *

TEA COFFEE

CRESS, MUSHROOM, AND LOBSTER BISQUE

¼ pound fresh mushrooms
3 tablespoons butter, divided
⅓ cup chopped water cress
1 tablespoon minced onion
¼ teaspoon celery seed
2 cups chicken broth
3 tablespoons flour
1 teaspoon salt
⅛ teaspoon pepper
1 cup light cream
½ cup milk
1 cup diced fresh cooked lobster meat
3 tablespoons dry sherry

Chop mushrooms fine; add 2 tablespoons butter, cress, onion, celery seed. Simmer, covered, for 5 minutes. Add chicken broth; simmer uncovered, for 10 minutes. Melt remaining 1 tablespoon butter; blend in flour, salt and pepper. Combine cream and milk; add. Stir over low heat until thickened. Add mushroom mixture, lobster meat, and sherry. Heat through. Makes 8 servings.

PÂTÉ BISCUITS
(soup accompaniment)

Make rich biscuit dough; roll about ⅛-inch thick; cut in 1½-inch rounds. On half the rounds place 1 measuring teaspoon minced chicken livers. Top with remaining rounds; crimp edges together. Brush tops with heavy cream. Bake in hot oven, 450°, until golden brown, about 10 minutes.

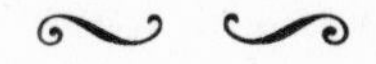

FRUIT SALAD MANDARIN

- 1 package (3 oz.) cream cheese
- 1 tablespoon mayonnaise
- ⅛ teaspoon salt
- 18 pitted dates
- 1 avocado
- ¼ cup lemon juice
- Salad greens
- 1 can (11 oz.) mandarin oranges

Mix cream cheese with mayonnaise and salt until smooth and creamy. Fill dates; chill. Peel and slice avocado crosswise, making rings; then dip in lemon juice. Place salad greens in center of plate; arrange stuffed dates on top. Around center, place avocado rings; fill each with mandarin orange segments. Garnish with salad greens. Serve with mayonnaise or French dressing. Makes 6 servings.

SHERRY DESSERT

- 2 8-inch sponge cake layers
- ¾ cup sweet sherry
- 1 cup whipping cream
- ½ teaspoon almond flavoring
- 2 tablespoons fine granulated sugar

Halve each cake layer crosswise to make 4 layers. Press 1 layer into 7-inch mixing bowl; sprinkle with 3 tablespoons sherry. Whip cream, beating in flavoring and sugar. Spread ⅓ of the cream over cake layer in bowl. Add second layer, pressing gently yet firmly to make cake conform to shape of bowl. Sprinkle with 3 tablespoons sherry; spread with ⅓ of the cream. Repeat with third layer; top with fourth layer of cake. Chill several hours or overnight. Unmold; frost with additional whipped cream. Garnish with slivered toasted almonds.

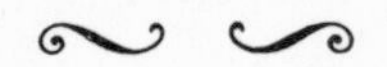

Menu

FORMAL DINNER

ASPARAGUS MUSHROOM SOUP

ROAST STUFFED SQUAB *

HEARTS OF PALM — CORN FRITTER PUFFS *

LIME SHERBERT

PEACH DESSERT OMELET *

TEA — COFFEE

ROAST STUFFED SQUAB

- 4 cleaned squabs (about 1 lb. each)
- 1½ cups butter, divided
- ½ pound mushrooms, minced
- 1 tablespoon minced onion
- 1 tablespoon cut chives
- ¼ teaspoon savory
- 2 tablespoons minced parsley
- 2½ teaspoons salt, divided
- ½ teaspoon pepper
- ½ teaspoon celery salt
- Dash Tabasco
- 4 cups soft bread crumbs
- 1 cup water
- ¼ teaspoon marjoram
- ¼ teaspoon rosemary

Heat oven to 500°. Wash squabs; pat dry. Melt ½ cup of the butter in skillet; add mushrooms and onion; cook until soft but not brown. Add another ½ cup butter, chives, parsley, 2 teaspoons of the salt, pepper, celery salt, Tabasco and crumbs. Mix well. Stuff squab with this mixture. Truss. Place, breast side up, on rack in shallow roasting pan. Melt remaining ½ cup butter; combine with water and herbs; pour over squabs. Roast at 500° for 15 minutes. Lower heat to 400°; roast 30 minutes longer, basting every 10 minutes with pan drippings. Makes 4 servings.

CORN FRITTER PUFFS

- 3 eggs, separated
- 1⅔ cups kernel corn, cut from cobs (cooked)
- ½ teaspoon seasoned salt
- ⅛ teaspoon pepper
- ¼ cup sifted, enriched flour
- 6 tablespoons salad oil

Beat egg yolks until light; stir in corn, salt, pepper and flour; fold in stiffly beaten egg whites. Drop by tablespoonfuls into hot salad oil. Cook on both sides until brown and done. Serve as a vegetable. Makes 6 servings.

PEACH DESSERT OMELET

6 eggs, separated
6 tablespoons water
1 teaspoon salt
2 tablespoons butter
2 cups sliced, sweetened fresh peaches

Heat oven to 325°. Beat egg whites with water and salt until whites are stiff and shiny, but still moist and form peaks when beater is raised. Beat egg yolks until thick and lemon colored. Fold yolks lightly but thoroughly into whites. Heat butter in 10-inch skillet (with heat-resistant handle). Tip skillet to coat bottom and sides. Pour in omelet mixture. Cook over low heat about 5 minutes or until omelet is puffy and golden on underside. Bake at 325° about 12 to 15 minutes or until surface feels dry. Run spatula around inside of skillet. Cut partway through center at right angles to handle. Fold over at cut. Tip out onto a hot platter. Fill with sliced sweetened peaches. Sprinkle top with powdered sugar. Makes 4 servings.

Menu

INFORMAL DINNER

GRAPEFRUIT PIQUANT *

VEAL STEAK SUPRÊME *

POPPY SEED NOODLES

GREEN BEANS SHOE-STRING BEETS

AVOCADO SALAD

HOT ROLLS

ZABAGLIONE *

TEA COFFEE

GRAPEFRUIT PIQUANT

- 2 large grapefruit
- ¾ cup ketchup
- ½ teaspoon salt
- 2 tablespoons lemon juice
- 1½ tablespoons Worcestershire sauce

Peel grapefruit; separate into segments. Chill. Mix ketchup, salt, lemon juice and Worcestershire sauce. Chill. Arrange grapefruit sections in sherbet glasses; add cocktail sauce. Serve immediately. Makes 6 servings.

VEAL STEAK SUPRÊME

- ¼ cup flour
- 1 tablespoon paprika
- 1 teaspoon salt
- 1 veal steak, 3 lbs., 1½-inches thick
- 3 onions, sliced thin
- 3 tablespoons fat
- 1 cup water
- 1 cup dairy sour cream
- 2 tablespoons sherry
- ¼ teaspoon oregano

Combine flour, paprika, and salt; dredge veal thoroughly in this mixture. Cook onions in fat over low heat until soft and golden; remove from pan. Brown veal well on both sides in pan in which onions were cooked. Place onions on veal. Add any remaining flour mixture to pan, with water; cover; simmer until veal is tender, about 1 hour. Remove veal and onions to platter; keep warm. Add cream, sherry, and oregano to pan; stir to blend; heat to serving temperature. Pour over veal. Makes 6 servings.

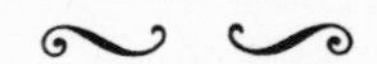

ZABAGLIONE

6 egg yolks
1½ cups sugar
4 teaspoons grated lemon peel
3 tablespoons lemon juice
1 cup Marsala wine

Beat egg yolks slightly in top of double boiler. Add remaining ingredients. Cook over boiling water, beating constantly with rotary egg beater until thick and fluffy, like whipped cream. Remove from hot water at once. Serve warm or chilled in dessert glasses. Makes 8 servings.

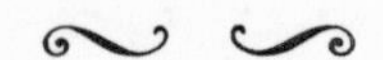

Menu

INFORMAL LUNCHEON

FRUIT CUP

CREAMED FINNAN HADDIE WITH DILL ON TOAST POINTS *

SAUTÉED CORN AND RED PEPPERS GREEN PEAS

HOT BAKING POWDER BISCUITS

JELLIED VIN ROSÉ *

THIN POUND CAKE SLICES

TEA COFFEE

CREAMED FINNAN HADDIE WITH DILL

1½ pounds finnan haddie
Milk
3 cups medium white sauce
1 tablespoon snipped fresh dill
Toast points

Cover finnan haddie with milk; bring slowly to a boil; lower heat and keep just below simmering for 20 minutes; drain. Use this milk in making white sauce; add salt sparingly, if any is needed. Break finnan haddie into chunks; add to white sauce with dill. Serve on toast points. Makes 6 servings.

JELLIED VIN ROSÉ

3 envelopes unflavored gelatine
3 cups vin rose, divided
½ teaspoon mace
3 cups boiling water
½ cup lemon juice
1½ cups sugar

Soften gelatine in 1 cup wine. Add mace and boiling water; stir until gelatine is dissolved. Add lemon juice, sugar, and remaining wine. Stir until sugar is dissolved. Pour into 7-cup mold. Chill until set. Unmold. Garnish with heavy cream.

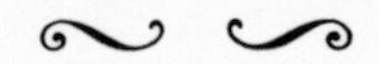

Menu

FORMAL HOLIDAY DINNER

OYSTERS ON THE HALF SHELL

ROAST GOOSE WITH APPLE-SESAME STUFFING *

COMPOTE OF PRUNES AND CHESTNUTS *

CREAMED ONIONS WITH NUTMEG   SWEET POTATOES GLACÉ

JELLIED CRANBERRY SAUCE

CELERY HEARTS   CARROT STICKS

BRANDIED MINCEMEAT PIE

PUMPKIN CHIFFON PIE

DEMITASSE

ROAST GOOSE WITH APPLE-SESAME STUFFING

1 goose (8 to 10 pounds, dressed weight)
2 packages stuffing mix
½ cup diced celery
¼ cup dried parsley flakes
4 tart apples, chopped
1½ teaspoons salt
2 teaspoons poultry seasoning
¼ teaspoon coarse black pepper
½ cup toasted sesame seeds *
½ cup giblet stock
2 tablespoons minced onion

Wash goose inside and out; pat dry. Cook giblets to make stock. (Use chopped giblets in gravy.) Prepare stuffing mix as directed on package. Add rest of ingredients; mix thoroughly. If stuffing is not moist enough, add a little more stock to taste. Stuff and truss goose; place on rack in large open roasting pan. Do not add water; do not cover. Roast at 325° for 4 to 4½ hours until thoroughly done. (If goose is very fat, prick skin lightly after first hour.) Makes 8 servings.

COMPOTE OF PRUNES AND CHESTNUTS

½ pound large prunes
1 piece stick cinnamon 2 inches long
1 tablespoon sugar
4 thick slices lemon
½ pound chestnuts

Soak prunes several hours or overnight in cold water to cover. Cook in same water, adding cinnamon, sugar, and lemon juice, until soft. Cool. Remove lemon slices and cinnamon; pit prunes and return to juice. Meanwhile, cut a deep slit in each

* *To toast sesame seeds:* Spread seeds in shallow pan. Toast in moderate oven, 350°, for 20 to 25 minutes.

chestnut. Cover chestnuts with water; boil for 20 minutes; drain. As soon as chestnuts are cool enough to handle, peel; cut in half; add to prunes. Serve hot as an accompaniment to goose or duckling. Makes 8 servings.

Menu

LATE SUPPER

CELERY STUFFED WITH ROQUEFORT CHEESE

AND RHINE WINE

SEA-FOOD MÉLANGE *

GRAPEFRUIT-AVOCADO SALAD

FRENCH DRESSING

CHOCOLATE MINT ICE CREAM

POUND CAKE

COFFEE

SEA-FOOD MÉLANGE

½ cup butter
½ teaspoon white pepper
½ teaspoon salt
¼ teaspoon dry mustard
¼ cup chopped onion
¼ cup chopped green pepper
1 cup cooked crab meat, flaked
1 cup cooked flaked lobster
½ cup Rhine wine

Melt butter in heavy saucepan or skillet; add seasonings, onion, and green pepper. Cook and stir five minutes, or until onions and pepper are tender. Add sea food; stir to coat well with sauce. Turn mixture into buttered 1-quart baking dish. Bake at 350° for 15 minutes. Turn heat off; add wine; stir; cover casserole. Close oven door and let dish stay ten minutes. Serve on toast points, crackers, or split and toasted rolls. Makes 4 servings.

Menu

FORMAL DINNER

CLAMS CASINO

CHICKEN CHABLIS *

GRILLED TOMATO HALVES SHOESTRING POTATOES

PICTURE PLATTER OF VEGETABLES

(LIMA BEANS, PEAS, GREEN BEANS, CAULIFLOWER)

BIBB LETTUCE WITH THOUSAND ISLAND DRESSING

SKY HIGH CHOCOLATE SOUFFLÉ *

CAFÉ BRÛLOT FLAMBÉ *

CHICKEN IN CHABLIS SAUCE WITH GRAPES

4 whole chicken breasts, boned
5 tablespoons butter, divided
2 teaspoons seasoned salt
½ pound mushrooms, sliced
2 tablespoons flour
1¾ cups milk
2 egg yolks, slightly beaten
¼ cup Chablis
1 cup seedless white grapes

Halve boned chicken breasts, making 8 pieces. Brown slowly in 3 tablespoons of the butter; remove to casserole; sprinkle with seasoned salt. Brown mushrooms in same pan. Add to casserole. Melt remaining butter; blend in flour. Add milk; cook and stir over low heat until smooth and thickened. Pour a little hot white sauce on egg yolks; mix well; return to remaining sauce; blend. Add wine. Pour into casserole. Bake at 350°, covered, for 20 minutes. Remove cover. Arrange grapes in center; bake, uncovered, for 10 minutes longer. Makes 4 servings.

SKY HIGH CHOCOLATE SOUFFLÉ

1 cup milk, divided
2 squares unsweetened chocolate
⅓ cup flour
¼ teaspoon salt
4 eggs, separated
⅓ cup sugar
2 teaspoons vanilla

Heat oven to 425°. Butter 1½-quart soufflé dish or casserole liberally. Coat bottom and sides with a little granulated sugar. Heat ½ cup of the milk and chocolate in double boiler until chocolate is melted. Beat smooth with egg beater. Mix flour and salt; stir in remaining milk; stir into chocolate mixture; cook and stir until very thick. Remove from heat; beat until smooth. Add egg yolks one at a time to chocolate mixture, beating well after each addition; cover; let stand. Beat egg whites until peaks form when beater is raised. Add sugar slowly, continuing to beat until stiff. Fold in chocolate mixture and vanilla. Pour into soufflé dish. Bake 25 to 27 minutes or until knife inserted in center comes out clean. *Serve at once.* Makes 6 servings.

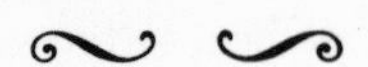

CAFE BRÛLOT FLAMBÉ

6 pieces of lump sugar
8 whole cloves
1 1-inch cinnamon stick
Peel from 1 lemon, cut up
4 jiggers cognac brandy
1 quart hot demitasse coffee

Place all ingredients, except coffee, in chafing dish. Ignite cognac with match and stir ingredients until well blended. After a minute or two, slowly pour in the hot black coffee and continue to stir. (In winter, heat brandy before using.) Makes 6 to 8 servings. To serve, strain into Brûlot or demitasse cups.

Section Three

BAHIA MAR

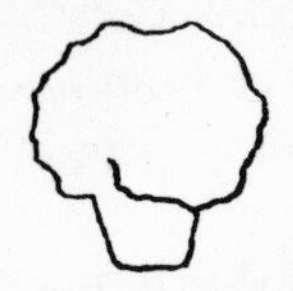

My florida candlelight is somewhat similar to its Westchester counterpart—with Candlelight, Crystal, and Garden Rooms, a small but varied garden overlooking the Intra-Coastal Waterway, a fountain, a gift shop, and a spacious cocktail lounge where one can sip drinks and munch delicious shrimps and other hors d'oeuvres while waiting to dine.

The clientele is excitingly varied. Millionaire yachtsmen rub shoulders with famous baseball players. Tourists mingle with Fort Lauderdale residents, college students mix with distinguished senior citizens. With such an assortment of customers I try to have something for everyone's taste on my bill of fare, and you will find that the following recipes reflect this variety.

Salads are naturally very important in the constantly sunny south. And baked stuffed shrimp is just about tops in demand at Bahia Mar. Here is a dish which makes excessive demands on the most ambitious housewife, but it's well worth it. I promise that the unusual sauce alone will draw applause. The fruits (coming from Kinsale) include mangoes and passion fruit, and the snow peas, bibb lettuce, strawberries, and watermelons are traditional favorites.

What might be termed staple dishes have always been "best-sellers" at my Candlelight restaurants and several are given here. These appeal strongly to the mighty New York Yankee ball players who dine so frequently at Bahia Mar during spring practice.

Just as in the case of the Westchester Candlelight, recipes which are employed to serve thousands can be used just as well for a small family. At least you know you're in good company when you use them.

Much of the success of the Bahia Mar Candlelight is due to the imaginative and satisfying culinary skill of Vincent Quiaioit, who presides over the kitchens, and has been our executive chef for 28 years.

CANDLELIGHT CREAM OF CHEESE SOUP

½ carrot
1 small onion
¼ cup butter
½ cup flour
2 cups chicken broth
½ cup Kraft Cheese Whiz
2 cups hot milk or light cream
Salt and pepper to taste

Mince carrot and onion; cook in boiling water until tender; drain. Melt butter; blend in flour. Add broth and Cheese Whiz; whip until creamy. Stir in hot milk, onion, and carrot. Season with salt and pepper; heat to boiling point, but do not boil. Serve at once. Makes 6 servings.

BAKED NESSELRODE PUDDING

½ cup butter
1 cup sugar
3 eggs
1 cup dark corn syrup
½ cup Nesselrode fruit mix
1 tablespoon rum
2 cups cake crumbs
½ cup flour
½ teaspoon baking soda
¼ teaspoon salt
1 cup buttermilk

Cream butter to consistency of mayonnaise. Add sugar gradually, continuing to cream until light and fluffy. Add eggs one at a time, beating well after each addition. Add corn syrup slowly, while beating. Add fruit mix, rum, and cake crumbs; mix well. Mix and sift flour, baking soda, and salt; add alternately with buttermilk. Pour into well-greased 10-inch-square pan. Bake at 350° for 45 to 50 minutes or until cake tester comes out clean. Cut into 12 squares. Serve warm with ice cream sauce.[1]

[1] *To make ice cream sauce:*

2 eggs	3 tablespoons lemon juice
1½ cups powdered sugar	1 cup heavy cream

Beat eggs until light; add sugar gradually, beating constantly. Add lemon juice. Whip cream; fold into egg and sugar mixture. Makes 12 servings.

BEEF STROGANOFF

2 pounds beef tenderloin, cut ¼″ thick in strips 2 or 3″ long	2 tablespoons flour
Salt	2 cups beef stock
Freshly ground pepper	2 tablespoons grated onion
½ cup butter, divided	1 cup dairy sour cream
	½ lb. mushrooms, sliced

Sprinkle meat with salt and pepper; let stand 1 hour at room temperature. Melt 4 tablespoons butter. Blend in flour until smooth. Gradually add beef stock, stirring constantly. Add onion. Blend in sour cream. Set aside. Sauté mushrooms in remaining butter 3 to 5 minutes. Remove; add to sauce. Sauté meat strips in same pan over high heat until well browned, adding more butter if necessary. Add meat to sauce. Cover; let simmer gently for 15 minutes. Serve immediately. Makes 6 servings.

ROCK CORNISH GAME HENS WITH WILD RICE STUFFING AND BRANDIED PEACHES

4 Rock Cornish Game Hens
½ cup wild rice
2 tablespoons pistachio nuts
2 tablespoons melted butter
3 cooked pork sausages, chopped
1 tablespoon minced onion
2 tablespoons minced celery
1 tablespoon brandy
Salt and pepper to taste
4 strips bacon
½ cup water
2 tablespoons lemon juice

Wash birds; pat dry. Rub cavities with lemon juice and a little salt. Cook wild rice according to package directions; add nuts, melted butter, sausage, onion, celery, brandy, salt and pepper. Stuff birds with wild rice mixture. Truss. Crisscross half-strips of bacon over each bird. Place in a shallow baking pan large enough so that birds do not touch each other. Pour water and lemon juice into pan. Roast at 500° for 15 minutes. Lower heat to 350°. Roast 45 minutes longer or until done. Baste with additional melted butter during last 15 minutes. Serve garnished with brandied peaches.[1] Makes 4 servings.

[1] *To make brandied peaches:*

8 large canned cling peach halves
¼ cup butter
¼ cup dark brown sugar
3 tablespoons brandy

Sauté peach halves gently in butter and sugar until lightly browned. Add brandy; let simmer for 5 minutes.

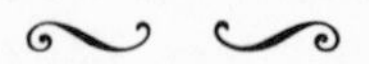

BAKED ACORN SQUASH WITH RUM

4 medium acorn squash
½ cup firmly packed light brown sugar
½ teaspoon cinnamon
½ cup butter, melted
½ cup rum

Cut squash in halves. Remove seeds and stringy pulp. Place cut side down in buttered baking pan. Bake at 400° for 30 minutes. Meanwhile, combine sugar, cinnamon, melted butter and rum. Turn squash halves cut side up. Spoon an equal amount of sugar mixture into each half. Return halves to oven. Bake about 30 minutes longer, brushing often with syrup from centers. Makes 8 servings.

SAUERKRAUT BALLS

2 large onions, finely chopped
1 bunch celery, finely chopped
3 tablespoons butter
1 pound ground lean beef
2 cups well-drained sauerkraut
2 cups flour
½ teaspoon salt
½ teaspoon Ac'cent
⅛ teaspoon pepper
2 eggs

Cook onion and celery in butter until brown. Add beef; cook over low heat about 8 minutes. Cool. Add sauerkraut (must be very dry), flour, seasonings and unbeaten eggs. Mix thoroughly. Shape into balls 1 inch in diameter. Fry in deep fat heated to 390° about 2 minutes or until brown. Drain on absorbent paper. Serve hot. Makes 20 to 25 servings.*

* This is a special concoction of Alfredo Orpesa, who has been with me for 26 years.

BAKED STUFFED SHRIMP

- 24 jumbo shrimp, cooked and cleaned
- 1 medium onion, minced
- 1 green pepper, minced
- 4 tablespoons butter, divided
- 1 can (7½ oz.) crabmeat, flaked
- 1 teaspoon dry sherry
- 1 teaspoon dry mustard
- 1 teaspoon Worcestershire sauce
- ½ teaspoon salt
- 2 tablespoons mayonnaise
- 1 cup basic medium white sauce
- Grated Parmesan cheese
- Paprika

Split shrimp and open flat. Cook onion and green pepper in two tablespoons butter until soft but not brown. Add crabmeat, sherry, mustard, Worcestershire sauce, salt, mayonnaise and white sauce; mix well. Stuff shrimp with crabmeat mixture. Dot with remaining butter. Sprinkle lightly with grated Parmesan cheese and paprika. Bake at 350° for 10 minutes. Makes 6 servings.

DEVILED CRAB

- ½ medium onion, finely chopped
- ½ green pepper, finely diced
- 3 tablespoons butter, divided
- 1 lb. fresh crabmeat, cooked and flaked
- 2 hard-cooked eggs, finely chopped
- 1 teaspoon dry mustard
- ½ teaspoon salt
- ½ cup mayonnaise
- 12 stuffed olives, chopped
- 1 tablespoon dry sherry
- 2 cups basic medium white sauce
- 1½ slices bread, crumbled

Cook onion and green pepper in two tablespoons butter until soft but not brown. Add crabmeat, mustard, eggs, salt, mayonnaise, olives, sherry, and white sauce; mix well. Spoon into 8 ramekins. Melt remaining butter; mix with bread crumbs; scatter on top of ramekins. Bake at 350° for 15 minutes. Usually served with Maine lobster sauce. Makes 8 servings.

BAKED PORK CHOPS WITH APPLE STUFFING

6 double loin pork chops
3 medium apples, finely chopped
½ cup brown sugar
1 teaspoon cinnamon
½ teaspoon nutmeg
3 cups hot water
1 carrot, finely chopped
1 medium onion, finely chopped
2 stalks celery, finely chopped
1 teaspoon salt
Few grains pepper

Cut deep pockets in chops. Combine apples, brown sugar, cinnamon and nutmeg; fill pockets with apple mixture. Place, stuffing side up, in baking pan. Pour water around chops; add carrot, onion, celery, salt and pepper to water. Bake in moderate oven, 350°, for 1½ hours. Thicken gravy if desired. Makes 6 servings.

CURRY OF LOBSTER

1 small onion, minced
½ green pepper, finely diced
2 tablespoons butter
1 teaspoon salt
2 tablespoons flour
1 tablespoon curry powder
1 slice lemon
1 tablespoon crushed pineapple
1 cup chicken broth
3 cans (5½ oz. each) lobster

Cook onion and pepper in butter until soft but not brown. Blend in salt, flour, and curry powder. Add lemon slice, pineapple, and chicken broth. Cook and stir over low heat until thickened. Add lobster; heat through. Serve on fluffy rice. Makes 6 servings.

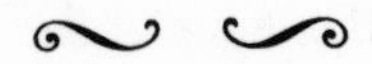

Section Four

WESTCHESTER CANDLELIGHT

The cookery of the Westchester Candlelight represents the culmination of my devotion to satisfying American dining tastes for over three decades.

Such recipes as that of the Patricia Murphy popover have remained standard through the depression, two World Wars, and the coming of the space age. Millions of these fluffy delicacies are eaten annually in Westchester and Bahia Mar, something over thirty million, to be exact. The same thing goes for the relish trays and the little cookies, and the petits fours which are served after the regular desserts and are available in the Jewel Box Gift Shop.

The lobster stuffed with shrimp and crabmeat—a perennial favorite of Candlelight guests—is sufficiently exotic to test the skill of the average cook, although it is not too difficult to prepare. Another great favorite of a multitude of diners is the rum chocolate cream pie. And although a few of the recipes are reasonably fancy, you will find simple but eminently satisfying dishes along with the recipes for ceremonial confections.

Supervising the preparation of this wide range of dishes is Burgos Gabriel, the executive chef of the Westchester Candlelight, who has been associated with me for 27 years.

Food editors and food fanciers are constantly amazed at that somewhat indefinable quality which stamps all Candlelight dishes. Between you and me, it is simply a matter of getting fine food to start with—good cuts of meat, fresh vegetables and fruit—and then preparing everything properly, using the best of condiments, real butter and, of course, loving care. There is no mystery to good cooking any more than there is to gracious entertaining. All it takes is patience, a dash of dedication, and a streak of showmanship.

This completes my selection of menus and recipes for dishes served to my many friends who come from all over the United States. Most of these recipes have never been shared before. From them I hope you will find new gustatory delight and inner satisfaction.

LOBSTER STUFFED WITH SHRIMP AND CRABMEAT

- 4 cans (4 oz. each) mushroom stems and pieces
- 1 medium onion, finely chopped
- ½ pound (2 sticks) butter, divided
- 13 oz. king crabmeat
- 1 pound shrimp, cooked and cleaned
- 3 lobsters (1½ to 2 pounds each), cooked
- 1 cup flour
- 1 tablespoon Ac'cent
- 1 tablespoon paprika
- ½ teaspoon salt
- ⅛ teaspoon black pepper
- 2½ cups milk
- 2 teaspoons Worcestershire sauce
- ½ cup dry sherry
- ⅓ cup shredded Parmesan cheese

Drain mushrooms. Cook onion in 3 tablespoons of the butter about 1 minute. Add mushrooms; cook over low heat about 5 minutes longer. Flake crabmeat; dice shrimp. Remove meat from lobsters; cut into chunks. Add crabmeat, shrimp, and lobster meat to mushroom mixture. Melt remaining butter; blend in flour, Ac'cent, paprika, salt and pepper. Add milk; cook and stir over low heat until smooth and thickened. Blend in Worcestershire sauce and sherry. Add lobster, crabmeat, shrimp, and mushroom mixture; mix well. Clean all cartilage from lobster shells. Fill each half heaping full with lobster mixture. Sprinkle with Parmesan cheese. Bake in hot oven, 425°, about 10 minutes or until golden brown and bubbly. Makes six servings.

GRILLED SWEETBREADS AND HAM WITH PINEAPPLE GLACÉ

- 4 pairs calves' sweetbreads
- 4 tablespoons lemon juice
- 2 stalks celery with leaves
- ½ cup chopped onion
- 6 to 8 peppercorns
- 8 slices Virginia ham
- 6 tablespoons butter, divided
- 8 canned pineapple slices
- 1 tablespoon pineapple juice
- ¼ cup honey

Wash sweetbreads under running cold water. Drain well. Place in a saucepan with water to cover. Add lemon juice, celery, onion, and peppercorns. Simmer for 20 minutes. Drain (save stock for gravy or soup). Cool. Remove skins and membranes from sweetbreads. Broil ham slices quickly. Sauté sweetbreads in 4 tablespoons butter about 5 minutes on each side. Sauté pineapple rings in remaining 2 tablespoons butter until lightly browned on both sides; place in shallow broiling pan and sprinkle with pineapple juice. Pour a little honey over each slice; broil, basting frequently until juice thickens. Place sweetbreads on ham slices; garnish with pineapple slices. Makes 8 servings.

PATRICIA MURPHY'S POPOVERS

Put ⅓ tsp. butter or Crisco in each muffin pan (or custard cup). Heat in oven 5 minutes while you are mixing batter.

- ¼ teaspoon salt
- 1 cup sifted flour
- 1 cup milk
- 2 eggs
- 1 tablespoon butter, melted (or Crisco)

Sift flour and salt into a bowl. Beat eggs with rotary beater, add milk, butter and sift in flour, beating only enough to make a smooth batter. Fill hot muffin pans (or custard cups) one-third full of the mixture. Bake in hot (450°) oven 30 minutes, then at 350° for 15 minutes or until firm, brown and popped. Keep oven door closed while baking. Makes 6 large popovers or 9 small.

CANDLELIGHT CHEESE CAKE

- 1 cup graham cracker crumbs
- 1¼ cups sugar, divided
- ¾ cup soft butter
- 1 pound soft cream cheese
- 4 whole eggs
- 2½ cups heavy cream
- Dairy sour cream

Combine crumbs, ½ cup sugar, and butter; press on bottom and sides of 8-inch spring form pan. Whip cheese until fluffy; beat in remaining sugar; continue beating until light and fluffy. Add eggs, one at a time, beating well after each addition. Stir in heavy cream. Strain through sieve into pan. Bake at 325° for 1 hour. Turn oven off; leave cheese cake in oven 1 hour. Remove from oven; let cool gradually to room temperature; chill. Top with layer of dairy sour cream. Wonderful served with thawed frozen strawberries, drained canned Mandarin Oranges or green seedless grapes on top of cheese cake.

BAKED MUSHROOM-STUFFED ONIONS

6 medium-sized yellow onions
1 can (4 oz.) mushroom stems and pieces
1 tablespoon finely chopped pecans
3 tablespoons butter
Salt and pepper
1 cup chicken consommé
Paprika

Peel onions and core, leaving shells about ½-inch thick. Pour boiling water over onions and skin will slip off easily. Cook cored onions in boiling water until almost tender. Meanwhile, chop raw onion pulp removed in coring. Chop mushroom stems and pieces. Sauté chopped raw onion, mushrooms, and pecans in butter about 10 minutes; season to taste with salt and pepper. Stuff onions with mushroom mixture. Arrange stuffed onions in shallow baking pan. Pour consommé around them. Sprinkle onions lightly with paprika. Bake at 350° about 10 minutes or until lightly brown and tender when pierced with a fork. Makes 6 servings.

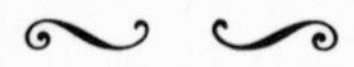

STUFFED BAKED APPLES

6 large Rome Beauty apples
⅔ cup seedless raisins
⅔ cup coarsely chopped walnuts
1 cup sugar, divided
1 cup hot water
1 3-inch piece stick cinnamon

Core apples, being careful not to cut through bottom; starting at stem end, peel halfway down. Cover raisins with boiling water; let stand 5 minutes; drain; combine with walnuts and

½ cup sugar. Fill apples with raisin mixture; place in baking pan. Pour hot water over apples. Pour remaining sugar over apples, leaving small mound of sugar on each. Place cinnamon stick in pan. Bake at 350° for 50 to 60 minutes or until apples are tender, basting occasionally with syrup in pan. When apples are done spoon any remaining syrup over them. Chill. Serve with plain or whipped cream. Makes 6 servings.

MISSISSIPPI PECAN PIE

3 eggs
⅔ cup sugar
Dash of salt
1 cup dark corn syrup
⅓ cup melted butter
1 teaspoon vanilla
1 cup pecan halves
1 9-inch unbaked pastry shell

Beat eggs thoroughly. Beat in sugar, salt, corn syrup, and melted butter. Add vanilla and pecans. Pour into unbaked pastry shell. Bake at 375° for 40 to 45 minutes or until knife inserted halfway between outside and center of filling comes out clean. Cool pie before serving. Serve with whipped cream topping, if desired.

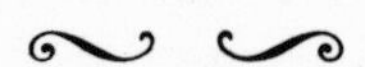

LITTLE SHRIMP PIES WITH FLAKY CRUST

1 lb. medium-sized shrimp
6 tablespoons butter, divided
2 tablespoons dry sherry
1 teaspoon salt
1 teaspoon grated onion
4 tablespoons flour
2 cups milk
Rich pastry (enough for 1 crust 9-inch pie)

Sauté shrimp in 2 tablespoons of the butter and sherry. Add salt. Melt remaining butter; add onion; cook 3 minutes. Blend in flour. Add milk; cook and stir over medium heat until thickened and smooth. Add shrimp. Spoon into four individual pie plates, 6 inches in diameter. Roll out pastry; cut in 6-inch circles. Place on pies. Cut slits in top to allow escape of steam. Bake at 350° for 25 to 30 minutes or until pastry is golden brown. Makes 4 servings.

RUM CHOCOLATE CREAM PIE

4 cups milk, divided
2 tablespoons butter
1 cup sugar
2 squares unsweetened chocolate, melted
6 tablespoons cornstarch
4 egg yolks, slightly beaten
2 tablespoons rum
½ teaspoon salt
1 10-inch baked pie shell
1 cup whipping cream

Combine ¾ cup milk, butter, and sugar. Stir over low heat until mixture comes to a boil. Add melted chocolate; mix well. Blend cornstarch to thin paste with a little of the cold milk; stir in remaining cold milk; add to chocolate mixture slowly while stirring. Cook and stir until well thickened. Cook for 10 minutes without stirring. Add hot mixture to egg yolks; mix well; return to saucepan; add salt, cook and stir for 1 minute. Remove from heat; add rum. Spoon into baked pie shell. Chill until firm. Whip cream; swirl on pie. Shave bittersweet chocolate on top in long strips.

ASPARAGUS MUSHROOM SOUP

- 1 dozen stalks asparagus, cut in 1-inch pieces
- 3 tablespoons butter
- 1 medium-sized onion, finely chopped
- 12 fresh medium-sized mushrooms, chopped
- 2 tablespoons flour
- 1½ cups chicken broth
- 1 cup milk
- ½ cup asparagus water
- Salt and pepper to taste
- 1 tablespoon dry sherry

Cook asparagus until tender; drain, reserving ½ cup asparagus water. Melt butter. Cook onion in butter until soft but not brown. Add mushrooms; cook until golden brown. Blend in flour. Combine chicken broth, milk, and asparagus water; stir until blended; let simmer 15 minutes (do not boil). Season to taste. Add sherry and asparagus; heat to serving temperature. Makes 6 cups.

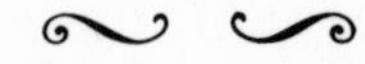

INDEX